ISBN 978-1-330-14126-7
PIBN 10035875

1 MONTH OF
FREE
READING

at

www.ForgottenBooks.com

By purchasing this book you are eligible for one month membership to ForgottenBooks.com, giving you unlimited access to our entire collection of over 1,000,000 titles via our web site and mobile apps.

To claim your free month visit:

www.forgottenbooks.com/free35875

English
Français
Deutsche
Italiano
Español
Português

www.forgottenbooks.com

Mythology Photography **Fiction**
Fishing Christianity **Art** Cooking
Essays Buddhism Freemasonry
Medicine **Biology** Music **Ancient
Egypt** Evolution Carpentry Physics
Dance Geology **Mathematics** Fitness
Shakespeare **Folklore** Yoga Marketing
Confidence Immortality Biographies
Poetry **Psychology** Witchcraft
Electronics Chemistry History **Law**
Accounting **Philosophy** Anthropology
Alchemy Drama Quantum Mechanics
Atheism Sexual Health **Ancient History**
Entrepreneurship Languages Sport
Paleontology Needlework Islam
Metaphysics Investment Archaeology
Parenting Statistics Criminology
Motivational

KING DAVID OF ISRAEL

A STUDY IN THE EVOLUTION OF ETHICS

BY

CHARLES CALLAWAY, M.A., D.Sc.

[ISSUED FOR THE RATIONALIST PRESS ASSOCIATION, LIMITED]

WATTS & CO.,
17, JOHNSON'S COURT, FLEET STREET, LONDON, E.C.
1905

CONTENTS

INTRODUCTION

THE object of this book is to present, in a form adapted for general readers, an impartial sketch of the state of morality among the Hebrew people for some centuries after they had settled down as an organized people among the nationalities of Western Asia. Such a period was necessarily transitional. The customs and modes of thought characteristic of a nomadic life were being slowly transformed under the influence of a new environment. A loose assemblage of clans had gained a footing among the hills on the western side of the Jordan valley, and the pressure of circumstances had forced them into a somewhat discordant unity under the rule of despotic kings. The Kingdom of Israel took its place side by side with the petty monarchies of Edom, Moab, and Ammon, which maintained a precarious existence on or near the great roadways between the mighty empires occupying the valleys of the Euphrates and the Nile. It entered into diplomatic relations, it engaged in trade and commerce, and it gradually acquired, with the assistance of its older neighbours, the habits of semi-civilised life.

This change of conditions necessarily produced changed ethics. A wider range of interests gave rise to new maxims of conduct. But the instincts and habits of the nomad were not at once destroyed. They survived, in decreasing strength, amid the integrating and ameliorating influences of a larger life. Such a period is therefore of much interest to the student of ethics, and this interest is increased tenfold by the great part which the Hebrews were destined to take in the evolution of the three great religions which have dominated the Western world.

There would seem to be no better mode of investigating the morals of a nation at any epoch than to analyze the character of one of its members who has become specially distinguished for holiness, and to ascertain the estimate formed of him by the people of his own age. This estimate will obviously be constructed under the influence of the current moral ideas, and will be a fair test of their quality. Simon Stylites, for example, acquired the title of Saint by standing on the top of high pillars for thirty-seven years, and undergoing during that period unspeakable hardship and suffering. A later time counts among its holy ones practical philanthropists like William Wilberforce and Florence Nightingale. In the former period the saint does nothing for his fellow-men but set them a useless, if not pernicious, example; and we may infer that, in his time, a barren asceticism was reckoned among the highest ethical qualities, as it is to-day in Hindu religion. In the age of Wilberforce a truer conception of morals had come into vogue.

For the purpose of this book, King David is

selected as the typical good man of the earlier centuries of the Hebrew monarchy. In both the Old and the New Testaments he stands upon a pinnacle of heroic saintliness. He is selected for the kingship by God as " a man after his own heart "[1] (1 Sam. xiii. 14). This description is endorsed by the apostolic authority of Paul (Acts xiii. 22). So lofty is the Davidic ideal that to be " Son of David " was regarded as a distinctive title of the Messiah himself. David may therefore be fairly selected as the highest type of manhood and sainthood that could be produced in Palestine 3,000 years ago. His virtues were the virtues, and his vices were the vices, characteristic of the Hebrew people in the transitional epoch to which I have referred. If certain of his acts are commended (or condemned) by his contemporaries or early successors, we may assume that they were in accordance with (or contrary to) the current moral code.

C. C.

September, 1905.

---

[1] The Revised Version is used throughout this book.

PART I.

THE SOURCES OF OUR INFORMATION

OUR knowledge of the life and character of David must, in the main, be derived from the Bible. But this statement requires some elucidation. Between the Bible of the Salvation Army and the Bible of the *Encyclopædia Biblica* there is a wide difference. The former is the revealed Word of God, inspired and infallible in every jot and tittle; the latter is a miscellaneous literature, compounded of myth, legend, true history, history coloured by theological preconceptions, and doctrinal and ethical teaching of varying truth and value. According to the traditional school, the events recorded in the Scriptures are real events, and the persons described are real persons. The higher critics, on the other hand, pronounce so momentous an event as the Fall of Man to be a myth;[1] and, with respect to so prominent a personage as Abraham, it is declared by Canon Cheyne that his "real existence is as doubtful as that of other heroes,"[2] while the histories of the patriarchs are set down, by the Rev. Dr. Moore, as "pure legend."[3]

---

[1] *Enc. Bib.*, col. 8581.

[2] *Ibid*, col. 26.   [3] *Ibid*, col. 2076.

Between these two extremes the hypotheses vary indefinitely.

§ 1. *Theories of Inspiration Immaterial.*

It is not necessary for my main purpose that I should select any one theory of inspiration or non-inspiration. As regards the life and character of David, it is immaterial whether he really did or said a thing, or some other person living not long after wrote that he did or said so. It is, for example, recorded (1 Kings ii. 9) that David, on his dying bed, exhorted his son Solomon to put Shimei to death for the insults he had offered when the king fled before Absalom. If David really spoke these last words, he displayed a certain state of mind; but if they were put into his mouth by a Jewish author two or three centuries later, we infer that, in the opinion of pious Jews of that age, such words, spoken at such a time, were quite consistent with the saintly character of the hero-king. In either case, we learn that the virtue of forgiveness had not reached a high development among the Hebrews of the earlier monarchy.

While the degree of authority to be attached to the Biblical record is not material to my main argument, it will greatly assist our discussion if we can acquire clear ideas on certain questions of date and authorship.

§ 2. *Dates of the Books.*

The question of dates has an obvious bearing

upon the evolution of Hebrew ethics. If, for example, the Pentateuch was written before the time of David, as we were taught a generation ago, we are forced to conclude that the saintly monarch had fallen below the ethical standard of preceding ages. Thus, it is written in Deuteronomy (xxiv. 16) that "the fathers shall not be put to death for the children, neither shall the children be put to death for the fathers: every man shall be put to death for his own sin." Yet we read (2 Sam. xxi. 1–14) that, when the Gibeonites demanded the punishment of seven of the sons and grandsons of Saul for the crime of their ancestor against the Gibeonites, David replies, " I will give them," "and they hanged them in the mountain before the Lord." Had the more merciful law of Deuteronomy been known to David, it is unlikely that he would have wilfully transgressed it. It is also clear that this Deuteronomic command was unknown to the writer of the above passage, for he states that the three years' famine (ver. 1) was a punishment for Saul's offence, and that, after the execution of the seven men, "God was intreated for the land " (ver. 14). The hanging of Saul's descendants was therefore regarded in the time of the author of the passage as in accordance with a severer divine law. Such a commandment is found in Deuteronomy (v. 9), where Yahweh[1] is declared to be "a jealous God, visiting the iniquities of the fathers upon the

[1] Inaccurately translated "the Lord." The spelling "Yahweh" is preferred by scholars to "Jehovah."

children, and upon the third and upon the fourth generation of them that hate me." The more just law is the product of a later age, when the teaching of the prophets held up higher moral ideals. The new ethical theory is, in fact, formulated by Jeremiah (xxxi. 29, 30) as an advance upon an older maxim: " In those days they shall say no more, The fathers have eaten sour grapes, and the children's teeth are set on edge. But everyone shall die for his own iniquity: every man that eateth the sour grapes, his teeth shall be set on edge."

Ezekiel also works out this new conception with great elaboration in chapter xviii.: "What mean ye that ye use this proverb concerning the land of Israel, saying, The fathers have eaten sour grapes, and the children's teeth are set on edge? As I live, saith the Lord God, ye shall not have occasion any more to use this proverb in Israel." And then Ezekiel goes on through many examples to insist upon the law that "the soul that sinneth, it shall die; the son shall not bear the iniquity of the father, neither shall the father bear the iniquity of the son."

That the higher ethics of Deuteronomy xxiv. 16 is the product of the prophetic age is admitted by modern criticism. Even so conservative a thinker as Robertson Smith writes: "As a matter of historical fact, the law continues the work of the prophets."[1] We may, therefore, safely conclude that this higher teaching was

---

[1] *The Old Testament in the Jewish Church* (1881), p. 306.

unknown in the time of David, but belongs to a later age. It accordingly falls naturally into its place as an example of more advanced ethical development.

It is evident from such considerations as the above that the traditional interpretation of the Bible is inadmissible. We may, I think, accept with confidence the more moderate conclusions of the higher criticism. The following summary of these will be sufficient for this purpose :—

(a) The books of the Pentateuch are of composite origin, consisting of writings of various dates. The oldest parts are contributed by writers known as the Judaic and the Ephraimitic (J and E), or the Yahwist and the Elohist. A later phase of thought appears in the "Book of the Law," discovered in the reign of Josiah. It forms part of Deuteronomy, and is called "D." Later additions known as the Priestly Code (P) are not earlier than the Captivity, and were promulgated by Ezra and Nehemiah. "It is an established fact of modern Biblical research that the Pentateuch, or the Five Books of Moses in the shape in which we have them, cannot have originated before the time of Cyrus the Younger, who led the 10,000 Greeks against his brother, Artaxerxes II., and was killed in the battle of Cunaxa, 401 B.C."[1]

(b) A great part of the Books of Samuel and Kings was probably written prior to the Captivity.

[1] *Bibles Within the Bible*, Dr. Paul Haupt, p. 4.

(c) The Books of Chronicles date about 250 B.C.

(d) The Psalms cover several centuries, probably few or none of them being pre-Exilic.

(e) The prophets of the eighth century B.C. introduced an advanced moral element into Hebrew literature, their teaching being reflected into records attributed to earlier periods.

The bulk of the history of David's life is furnished by J, who probably wrote in the ninth century B.C. Several chapters are supplied by E, and are written a century or two later. They are in part duplicate accounts of events recorded by J. E also contributes a part of the narrative of David's fight with Goliath, portions of the romantic story of the friendship between David and Jonathan, Michal's device to save David's life, David's visit to Nob, the Nabal incident, Saul's adventure with the witch of Endor, the chapter on David's desire to build a house for Yahweh, and some small insertions here and there. To D are attributed a few short intercalations. The latest insertions (2 Sam. xxi.–xxiv.) are interposed in J's narrative after the Books of Samuel and Kings had been separated.

§ 3. *Did David Write Psalms?*

The writers of the Hexateuch (Pentateuch and Joshua) are unknown, and for the purpose of this book their anonymity is not material. It is, however, of the first consequence that we should ascertain whether David wrote the Psalms that bear his name. If he did, we are furnished with important evidence bearing on his character. If he did not, we are thrown back upon the narratives in 1 Sam. xvi.–1 Kings ii., 1 Chron. x.–xxix., and occasional references in other books.

It is admitted that the titles of the Psalms have no authority, and it would be a waste of time to argue the matter. We must be guided by the internal evidence. Out of 150 Psalms, seventy-three are ascribed to David by their titles in the Hebrew text. In some of these there are references that distinctly negative a Davidic authority. The following examples are the most decisive. They are given by W. Robertson Smith[1]:—

xiv. 7. "O that the salvation of Israel were come out of Zion! When the Lord bringeth back the captivity of his people, then shall Jacob rejoice, and Israel shall be glad." This verse stamps the Psalm as written during the Exile.

xx. This Psalm is "not spoken by a king, but addressed to a king by his people." The Lord's "anointed" is mentioned in the third person (ver. 6); and in the last verse, "Save, Lord" (or in the margin, "O Lord, save the King"), "let the king answer us when we call," the petitioner is distinctly another than the king himself.

xxi. The prayer of this Psalm is also offered for, not by, a king.

[1] *Loc. cit.*, 193–211.

xxvii. The reference to the "temple" (ver. 4) stamps the Psalm as not earlier than Solomon. Furthermore, the latter part is appropriate only to a person in dependent circumstances. A great and successful king would not lament that his father and mother had forsaken him (ver. 10), or invoke protection from "false witnesses" (ver. 12).

xxxiv. The title of this Psalm refers to David feigning madness "before Abimelech." This appears to be a mistake for "Achish," for Abimelech was contemporary with Abraham. Such careless editing of itself excites suspicion. Also the ideas of the Psalm are quite inappropriate. The writer is a "poor man," who offers to teach his readers "the fear of the Lord," and who exalts the merit of "a broken heart" and "a contrite spirit."

xxxvii. This is in the same vein as xxxiv. Both the thoughts and expression are similar. The words "Depart from evil and do good" are identical in both.

cxxii. "For there are set thrones for judgement, the thrones of the House of David" (ver. 5) clearly could not have been written before those thrones and that house had come into existence.

cxliv. The Psalmist prays (vers. 10, 11), "Who rescueth David, his servant, from the hurtful sword. Rescue me." David and he are, therefore, different persons.

Perhaps the strongest evidence that David did not write the Psalms attributed to him is found in their advanced moral ideas; but this cannot be used as an argument in the present stage of our inquiry.

Canon Driver[1] works out the problem on similar lines. He remarks that frequently "the title is contradicted by the contents of the Psalm to which it is prefixed." Thus Psalm lii. is said to refer to Doeg, when, in fact, it describes a rich and powerful man, a persecutor of the righteous, whose pride will lead him to destruction, while the Psalmist "will flourish as a green olive tree in the house of God." Again, Psalm lviii. is a condemnation of unjust judges, whom, as king, David had-t power to remove. Yet he is represented as appealing to God to "break their teeth," and otherwise punish them.

Canon Driver concludes that "the majority of the 'Davidic' Psalms are certainly not David's." All the evidence, he considers, converges to the conclusion that these Psalms "spring from many periods of Israelitish history," and that "they set before us the experiences of many men, and of many ages of the national life." Whether any of the Psalms commonly assigned to David were really composed by him is a question which Driver regards as still uncertain.

Canon Cheyne[2] goes further than Robertson Smith and Canon Driver. He writes: "That

---

[1] *Introduction to the Literature of the Old Testament* (1892), pp. 851–367.

[2] *Enc. Bib.*, col. 8961.

there are no pre-Exilic Psalms, nor ascertainable
fragments of such Psalms, is for us at least
quite certain." It is not necessary for my
purpose that I should discuss Professor Cheyne's
conclusion, which he supports with a great
wealth of learning. It is sufficient for me that
the Davidic origin of many of the Psalms which
bear his name has been absolutely disproved.
The remainder, or some of them, may have
been composed by him; but of this there is no
proof, and the probabilities are all against it.

PART II.

THE REAL DAVID

SINCE we cannot extract from the Psalms any reliable information on the opinions and emotions of David, we are for the most part restricted to the historical books. It is reasonable to believe that, the nearer a writer lived to the actual period of David's life, the more likely was he, *cæteris paribus*, to be accurately informed of what the king said and did. For this reason we can attach but a secondary importance to the Books of the Chronicles. David died about the year 970 B.C., and the Chronicler probably did not write before 250 B.C. A period of 700 years, especially in an uncritical age, would lend itself to the growth of legend. That the Chronicler permitted his imagination undue liberties is admitted by the most moderate critics. The question will, however, be discussed in my section on " The Growth of the Ideal."

We shall, therefore, take as the basis of our knowledge of David's life and character the narrative contained in 1 Sam. xvi.–1 Kings ii. David's brilliant reign must have made a vivid impression upon the public imagination, and writers would be eager to chronicle his glorious career. With the reign of Solomon came in the

Deuteronomic method, in which true history
is subordinated to moral and religious purposes.
The life of David is not, indeed, free from
Deuteronomic colouring, but in the main it
presents the appearance of a genuine chronicle.
David's adventures as an outlaw, the combination of warlike prowess and political intrigue by
which he obtains the crown of united Israel, his
wars with surrounding nations, the conspiracies
which trouble his later years, the griefs that
embitter his domestic life, form the main
features of a biography which impresses the
reader as unexaggerated and natural. The
candour with which the writers narrate the sins
and defects of their hero is another test of their
veracity, though we must keep in mind that
many things that appear wrong to us were not
so regarded in David's age. Our impression of
the truthfulness of the records is greatly deepened
by their comparative freedom from the mira-
culous. The stupendous wonders of the Books
of Joshua and Judges compel our scepticism; and
again, in an age later than David's, the careers
of Elijah and Elisha, glooming weird and awful
with supernatural wonders, puzzle the critical
faculty to unravel the fact from the fiction. It
is otherwise with David's life. Save for the
communications with Yahweh by means of the
oracle, and the interventions of the national god
in David's battles, there is little that need be
rejected as inconsistent with natural law. These
personal relations with the national deity are
but the commonplaces of the history of three

millenniums ago. The Moabite stone tells us that
King Mesha gained his victories by the aid of
Chemosh;[1] and an Assyrian inscription[2] by
Shalmanezer, engraved on the rocks of Armenia,
declares: " By the supreme help which Assur,
the Lord, gave me......I fought......." This
theological colouring still tinges Semitic modes
of expression. Sir Samuel Baker[3] tells us:
" The conversation of the Arabs is in the exact
style of the Old Testament. The name of God
is coupled with every trifling incident in life.
Should a famine affect the land, it is expressed in
the stern language of the Old Testament, ' The
Lord has sent a grievous famine upon the land,'
or ' The Lord called for a famine, and it came
upon the land.' So, if there come a time of
special fertility among the flocks, the prosperity
is regarded as a blessing upon the people for
their good deeds. Suggestions in dreams are
regarded by these Arabs as ' the voice of the
Lord,' and the dreamer would affirm that ' God
had appeared to him in a dream, and said so and
so.' " We need not, therefore, reject Biblical
accounts of David's life and actions on the
ground that they are not expressed in the severe
naturalism of modern civilisation. We do not
refuse to believe that Mesha defeated Omri
because he tells us that Chemosh helped him to
do so. So, too, we may logically accept the
fact of David's victory at Baal-perazim, even
though the statement is prefaced by Yahweh's

[1] Sayce's *Fresh Light from the Ancient Monuments*, p. 69.
[2] *Ibid*, p. 102.   [3] *Nile Tributaries*, pp. 129-181.

command that he should "Go up." It is not difficult to separate the theological setting from the historical truth. We do so in Herodotus and Livy, and we may do so here.

In the following pages I shall not attempt a life of David; but shall touch only, or mainly, upon those incidents that throw light upon his moral and religious character, the latter only as it is related to the former.

§ 1. *Entrance upon Public Life.*

Two accounts are given of this event. In the first (1 Sam. xvi. 14–23) David is called in to play the harp before Saul to drive away his fits of insanity. David is described (ver. 18) as "a son of Jesse the Bethlehemite, that is cunning in playing, and a mighty man of valour, and a man of war, and prudent in speech, and a comely person." The second narrative describes him (1 Sam. xvii. 42) as "but a youth, and ruddy, and withal of a fair countenance," and he is brought into notice as the champion of Israel against Goliath of Gath. Such a stripling as this could hardly have been "a mighty man of valour, and a man of war." Indeed, when challenged by Saul to vindicate his fitness to fight the giant, he says no word about his experience in battle, but describes his prowess in killing the lions and bears that threatened his father's flocks. Furthermore, when Saul sees David going forth to fight the Philistine, he does not know who he is (xvii. 55), though, according to the first account, he was his own armour-bearer.

The two narratives are, therefore, inconsistent with each other.

It would seem that the second account is the less trustworthy. Indeed, the statement that David slew Goliath is contradicted by 2 Sam. xxi. 19, where we read that Goliath the Gittite was slain by "Elhanan, the son of Jaare-oregim the Bethlehemite." This must be the same Goliath, for he also is from Gath (Gittite is the ethnic of Gath), and to both is applied the description, "the staff of whose spear was like a weaver's beam." The critics regard the Elhanan tradition as the older. Furthermore, large portions of David's fight with Goliath are omitted in the Septuagint version of the event. It is, therefore, highly probable that the picturesque combat with Goliath was introduced by a late writer to illustrate David's zeal for Yahweh.

Falling back upon the more trustworthy tradition, we conclude that David's appearance in public life is not made until he has reached manhood, and has already acquired repute as a warrior. He is received into Saul's favour, and becomes his armour-bearer.

§ 2. *Marriage with Michal* (1 Sam. xviii. 20–29).

The way in which David wins his wife is characteristic of a barbarous age. Saul waives the payment of the usual purchase-money on condition that David brings him a hundred foreskins of the Philistines, hoping that David, against whom he has conceived violent jealousy, will be killed in the enterprise. David, however, so highly appreciates the honour of being the King's son-in-law that he doubles Saul's demand. Assuming the justifiability of David's attack upon the Philistines, it must be admitted that the subsequent mutilation of their bodies was a brutal act, worthy only of a savage chieftain. That it was customary in David's time simply proves that in this respect the Hebrews had not risen above the practice of barbarians.

§ 3. *Was David an Idolater?* (1 Sam. xix. 11–17).

This quaint story of the trick by which Michal deceives the messengers whom Saul had sent to slay her husband is very suggestive. What were these " teraphim," which she dresses up to imitate the " sick " David ? Gesenius translates the word "*domestic gods*, as if Penates, of the Hebrews." In the passage in Genesis (xxxi. 19–35), in which Rachel steals and hides her father's " teraphim," they were claimed by Laban as his " gods " (ver. 30), and Jacob (ver. 32) also calls them " gods " (*Elohim*, Heb.; *Theoi*, Sept.). From a narrative in Judges (xvii. 5, xviii. 14–21) we learn that Micah " had a house of gods, and he made an ephod, and teraphim, and consecrated one of his sons, who became his priest." Micah's teraphim are, therefore, objects connected with religious rites, but their exact nature is not specified. That teraphim were used in divination is clearly stated in the prophets. Ezekiel (xxi. 21) writes : " For the King of Babylon stood at the parting of the ways, at the head of the two ways, to use

divination: he shook the arrows to and fro, he
consulted the teraphim, he looked in the liver."
In Zechariah (xx. 2) we read: "For the
teraphim have spoken vanity, and the diviners
have seen a lie." The teraphim were held to
be of religious value even as late as the pious
Hezekiah, for Hosea threatens (iii. 4): "For the
children of Israel shall abide many days without
king, and without prince, and without sacrifice,
and without pillar (obelisk or menhir), and
without ephod or teraphim."

These teraphim were probably images, resem-
bling in a general way the human form, otherwise the deception practised by Michal could
not have been successful. That they were
regarded as gods is fairly evident from the above
quotations. Did David worship them? I see
no reason to doubt it. We read (ver. 18) that
"Michal took the teraphim, and laid it (or them)
in the bed." There is no suggestion in the narrative that they were worshipped exclusively by
Michal. She was daughter of the Hebrew Saul,
not a heathen, and, like David, presumably
adored the national god, Yahweh. Had David
been zealous for the exclusive cult of Yahweh,
it is inconceivable that he should have permitted these idols to remain in his house. The
Deuteronomic law against idols was most severe.
It commands (Deut. xiii. 6–11) that if a man's
nearest relative, even the wife of his bosom,
entice him to "serve other gods"......"thou
shalt surely kill him." Again, the Second Commandment distinctly specifies: "Thou shalt

not make unto thee a graven image." These laws could not have been known to David, or he would not have kept idols in his house. They express the more advanced theology of a later age. In David's time, and for several succeeding centuries, as we learn from the histories of the Kings of Israel and Judah, the cult of Yahweh was accompanied by lower forms of worship, the survivals of ancient idolatries. We may conclude that David himself, whose busy life of warrior and statesman could have left him little time for profound reflection on religious subjects, was not in advance of the prevailing idolatry of his age. He could, therefore, have had little conception of the advanced religious and ethical ideas attributed to him in the Book of Psalms.

§ 4. *David's Unveracity with Jonathan* (1 Sam. xx. 5–8).

David is in fear of Saul. To excuse his absence from the feast of the new moon, he asks Jonathan to tell his father a lie. Jonathan does so. He says (vv. 28, 29) : " David earnestly asked leave of me to go to Bethlehem : and he said, Let me go, I pray thee; for our family hath a sacrifice in the city; and my brother, he hath commanded me to be there; and now, if I have found favour in thine eyes, let me get away, I pray thee, and see my brethren. Therefore, he is not come unto the King's table." Jonathan garnishes David's untruth with additions of his own, and goes through his task glibly enough. There is no suggestion in the narrative that the deception was thought to be unjustifiable.

§ 5. *The Covenant with Jonathan* (xx. 8, 16–18, 42).

David's friendship with Jonathan brings out a more pleasing feature of David's character. The comrades pledge themselves to show kindness not only to each other, but to their respective descendants. Jonathan proves his goodwill to David by warning him of Saul's designs upon his life. David is not unmindful of his pledges. In after years, when he wears the crown of Israel, he shows kindness to Jonathan's son, Mephibosheth; and when he surrenders the descendants of Saul to the vengeance of the Gibeonites, he makes an exception in favour of Mephibosheth.

§ 6. *The Deception of Ahimelech, and its Murderous Consequences* (1 Sam. xxi. 1–9; xxii. 6–23).

David, fleeing from Saul, comes to Nob to Ahimelech, the priest, and asks for refreshment. He deceives the priest with an untruth, alleging that he was on the King's business, and obtains some of the shewbread. He thus involves Ahimelech in the penalties of treason. Doeg reveals the truth to the King. Ahimelech is sent for, and brought before Saul, but he denies the accusation (xxii. 15). This untruth does not deceive the King, who expresses no surprise at the mendacity of the holy man—a significant indication of the unveracity of the age. The royal vengeance falls heavily upon Ahimelech and all associated with him. Fourscore and five priests are slain. "And Nob, the city of the priests, smote he with the edge of the sword, both men and women, children and sucklings, and oxen and asses and sheep, with the edge of the sword" (ver. 19). All this crime and misery_v was caused by David's deceit and selfishness.

Reference is made to this event in the New Testament (Matt. xii. 3, Mark ii. 25). The example of David in eating the shewbread is quoted as a justification for the conduct of the disciples in plucking the ears of corn on the Sabbath. It is curious and significant that the ethical aspect of David's behaviour has fallen out of sight, and the attention of the disciples is directed to David as transgressing an unimportant ritual law.

§ 7. *Seeks Refuge in Gath: his Crimes while there* (1 Sam. xxi. 10–15, xxvii. 1–xxviii. 2, xxix. 2–11).

According to the critics, the longer narrative (J) is of date prior to 800 B.C., and the short account (xxi. 10–15) is by a much later writer, who thought that the older account reflected on David's patriotism, and who accordingly substituted a less objectionable story. This later version need not detain us. The feigned madness is merely another example of the ease with which David fell into deceit; but, under the circumstances, it is not perhaps to be severely reprobated. The following incidents in the longer account are worthy of notice :—

(a) David's raid upon the Geshurites, the Girzites, and the Amalekites (xxvii. 8–12).

It would be difficult to find in history anything more atrocious than the deeds here described. "David smote the land, and saved neither man nor woman alive." This would be bad enough if it were done in the heat of combat; but this excuse is not offered. David bluntly acknowledges that these murders were perpetrated deliberately, and for selfish motives. He tells us (ver. 11) that he did these things "lest they should tell on us, saying, So did David, and so hath been his manner all the while he hath dwelt in the country of the Philistines." Further comment is needless.

(b) His deceit to Achish.

He cloaks the wickedness just described with a lie. When Achish inquired, "Whither have ye made a raid to-day?" David replied, "Against the South of Judah, and against the South of the Jerahmeelites, and against the South of the Kenites," thus pretending that he had been fighting against the enemies of Achish. He worked his deception so well that the king was completely hoodwinked. This account, it must be remembered, was written by Hebrews, admirers of their hero-king, and it is written without any hint that such conduct was worthy of reprobation.

David keeps up the deception of his protector to the end. When Achish, at the request of the lords of the Philistines, refuses to permit him to join the Philistine army against the Israelites,

David, with affected innocence, remonstrates:
"But what have I done? and what hast thou
found in thy servant so long as I have been
before thee unto this day, that I may not go and
fight against the enemies of my lord the king?"
(xxix. 8). Achish replies that David was in his
sight "as an angel of God." The lords, however, were wiser than their king, and refused to
give David the opportunity of a second treason.

(c) Did David worship foreign gods?

This question may seem unnecessary to those
who hold the traditional view of David's devotion
to the worship of Yahweh. But certain considerations throw doubt upon this theory. The
deities of Canaan in David's time were tribal or
national, and Yahweh was no exception. He was
the God of Israel in the same sense as Chemosh
was the god of the Moabites. To Israelites every
country outside their own was "unclean," and the
worship of Yahweh could not be celebrated in it.
This belief is curiously illustrated in a later age
by the story of Naaman and his leprosy (2 Kings
v. 17). "And Naaman said, If not, yet I pray
thee let there be given to thy servant two mules'
burden of earth ; for thy servant will henceforth
offer neither burnt offering nor sacrifice unto
other gods, but unto the Lord." This clearly
implies that Yahweh could be adored only on his
own (Israelitish) soil; and, since Naaman lived
in a foreign country, he could worship Israel's
god only on a patch of Yahweh's earth, or
perhaps at an altar composed of it. Of course,
wider conceptions arose in a later age, when

Judah was transplanted to Babylonia; but even
then the legal sacrificial rites were in abeyance,
and were not renewed until the restoration.

The most distinct evidence of David's idolatry
is found in the second of the romantic descriptions of David's chivalrous refusal to take the
life of Saul (1 Sam. xxvi.). This account is
admitted by the critics to refer to the same
event as the narrative in chapter xxiv. Though
it comes later in the Bible, it is an older
tradition (J), and affords glimpses of a more
antique phase of thought. Verse 19 contains
this remarkable utterance: "If it be the Lord
that hath stirred thee up against me, let him
accept [*Heb.*, smell] an offering; but if it be the
children of men, cursed be they before the Lord;
for they have driven me out this day that I
should not cleave unto the inheritance of the
Lord, saying, Go, serve other gods." It appears
to be here distinctly suggested that banishment
from Israelitish soil compelled the service of
foreign gods. We, therefore, seem driven to
adopt the inference that when David sojourned
in Gath he was a worshipper of Dagon or
other Philistine god. This consideration
increases our difficulty in believing that he was
the fervid Yahweh-worshipper of the Book of
Psalms, and in accepting his authorship of any
of the Psalms attributed to him.

§ 8. *His Magnanimity to Saul* (1 Sam. xxiv.,
xxvi.).

It is a pleasure to turn from the darker aspects

of David's character to an act so generous as his refusal to take the life of his enemy when the opportunity came to him. Saul, however, was his personal foe, not the enemy of his people, and the ethical code which would justify the assassination of a foreigner, as in the case of Eglon by Ehud, would regard the private slaying of one of the same nation as a crime. David's motives were probably twofold. The reason he gives to Abner is likely to be a true one: " Destroy him not," he urges, " for who can put forth his hand against the Lord's anointed and be guiltless?" This reverence for the royal office was probably combined with a certain largeness of heart which scorned to take advantage of a defenceless foe. Such magnanimity was quite "in accordance with a chivalrous rule still common in Arabia."[1]

It is not improbable that David's generosity was reinforced by self-interest. He may well have had in view his probable accession to the throne, and would thus have a selfish reason for maintaining the inviolability of the royal person.

§ 9. David's non-ethical conception of Yahweh (1 Sam. xxvi. 19).

David knows that Saul is behaving unrighteously towards an innocent person, and yet he suggests that Saul's malignant purposes may have been stirred up by Yahweh. Thus he considers it possible that his god is the author

---

[1] Cheyne in *Enc. Bib.*, col. 1025.

of wickedness.   Furthermore, he proposes that, if Yahweh has done this evil thing, he should be induced to "smell an offering," and thus be placated.   There is no trace of moral character in such a deity as this.   And what are we to say of the ethical standard of the man who reveres and worships this deity?

§ 10.   *Oath to Saul, and its Violation* (1 Sam. xxiv. 21, 22).

Touched by David's generosity, Saul is repre-sented[1] (vv. 17–21) as repenting for his conduct to David, and acknowledging that David will be king.   Then he induces David to swear that he will spare Saul's posterity.   This oath was not kept.   At the demand of the Gibeonites, David gives up to them seven of Saul's descendants (2 Sam. xxi. 4–9), and they are hanged "in the mountain before the Lord."   David appears to have forgotten his oath, or he wilfully violates it to please the Gibeonites, and placate Yahweh, who is represented as conniving at David's perjury.   The whole transaction is ethically unpleasing.

§ 11.   *The Nabal Incident* (1 Sam. 25).

David, during his retreat from Saul's anger, passed the life of an outlaw.   He levied black-mail in return for protection against foreign

[1] This passage is an interpolation, and the story of the Gibeonites is also late; but the writer of the latter does not present to us a higher conception of David's character than we find in J.

raids. On one occasion he sends messengers
to ask Nabal for supplies, which are refused.
Now mark how David acts (vv. 13, 21, 22).
Because Nabal behaves churlishly, David sets
out to kill every male "of all that pertain to
him," including even the children. This atrocity,
we may presume, would have been carried out
had not Nabal's wife, Abigail, placated him with
a present and a flattering speech, backed up by
her fair face. David is brought to acknowledge
that his threatened vengeance would have been
"evil." The incident is but another example
of the ferocious spirit of the age and people,
and is quite in accord with the narrative which
represents Yahweh as rejecting Saul because he
had not executed "his fierce wrath upon Amalek"
(1 Sam. xxviii. 17, 18).

§ 12. *David's Equitable Division of the Spoil of*
the Amalekites (1 Sam. xxx. 24, 25).

This just division of the spoil was an advance
upon the rough methods of primitive ages, and
even upon the practices which have often disgraced much later times, when the fury of war
has overriden the claims of justice. The firm
spirit of the future king suppresses the selfish
impulses of his warriors, and establishes an
equitable rule, which was afterwards embodied
in the legislation attributed to Moses (Numb.
xxxi. 25, 26).

§ 13. *Politic Gifts to the Judahites* (1 Sam. xxx. 26–31).

With all his impulsiveness, David, like a true Jew, had a keen eye to the main chance. He must have been quite alive to the probabilities of the future. Whether or not we are to accept as genuine history Jonathan's abdication in David's favour of his claim to the succession, and Saul's acknowledgment of the divine appointment of David, we cannot doubt that his personal qualities and success in war marked him out as future king in a country where no royal house had yet been established. But a little judicious bribery could not fail to improve his chances. The time for this was well chosen. A decisive crisis was at hand. Saul's throne was tottering before the advance of the well-armed Philistines. It was well for David's prospects of a crown that he took no part in the great battle that was approaching. Had he done so, either success or failure would have meant failure for him. Fighting on the side of Israel's enemies, in victory or defeat he would have made himself hateful to the Hebrews. Deserting to his own people, as he would probably have done, their success would but have fixed the crown more firmly upon the head of his rival, while their overthrow would have involved him in the nation's fall. He stood aloof, and made himself friends with the mammon of unrighteousness. On the ruin and death of Saul, he was elected King of Judah.

§ 14. *Lamentation over Saul and Jonathan* (2 Sam. i.).

According to the narrative, David shows himself very loyal to the memory of his dead persecutor. When he received intelligence of the event, he rent his clothes, he wept and fasted; he put to death the messenger for having slain "the Lord's anointed"; and he pronounced an elegy on Saul and Jonathan. Whether this exquisite poem was really composed by David is by no means certain. It has an antique air, and, if it is not David's, is probably a product of the pre-prophetic age. It is quite unethical, and yields no glimpse of religious thought. Its pathos is that of a purely human heart, untouched by the influence of priest or prophet. If it is put into his mouth by a later writer, it indicates that, in the opinion of that writer, David's mind was not deeply saturated with pietistic emotion, and, therefore, was not the creator of the "Davidic" psalms.

§ 15. *Gratitude to the Men of Jabesh-Gilead* (2 Sam. ii. 4–7).

David's grateful message for the respect paid to the remains of his dead foe is worthy of a high civilisation. It contrasts very favourably with the behaviour of princes in times much nearer to our own—with, for example, the callous brutality of the sons of William the Conqueror and Henry II. on their fathers' death, and with the ignoble spitefulness of Charles II. to the

remains of Cromwell.   It is, of course, possible
that David's gracious message to the men of
Jabesh-Gilead was prompted by a desire to win
their support in his somewhat precarious position as newly-elected King of Judah ; but the
act is quite in accord with his chivalrous conduct
to Saul in the wilderness of Ziph.

§ 16. *Joab's Murder of Abner, and David's Condemnation* (2 Sam. iii. 27–39).

David distinctly reprobates the assassination
of Abner as " wicked."   It was perpetrated not
only in revenge, but through personal jealousy
of Abner's new influence with the king.   David,
however, though he condemns, cannot punish.
The royal power in Hebrewdom was not yet
sufficiently consolidated to enforce justice against
powerful subjects.   David washes his hands of
all share in the deed, and invokes the vengeance
of Yahweh upon the guilty man and upon his
family.   His curse (ver. 29), " Let it [the blood
of Abner] fall upon the head of Joab, and upon
all his father's house; and let there not fail
from the house of Joab one that hath an issue,
or that is a leper, or that leaneth on a staff, or
that falleth by the sword, or that lacketh bread,"
is quite in accordance with the primitive idea
that all the kin are responsible for the act of one
of its members, and Yahweh, the head of the
kin,[1] is called upon to execute the vengeance.

---

[1] W. Robertson Smith, *The Religion of the Semites*, pp. 53, 54.

§ 17. *The Assassination of Ish-bosheth* (iv. 5–12).

David's punishment of the murderers of Saul's heir and successor is of a piece with his execution of the Amalekite who claimed to slay Saul on Mount Gilboa. The basis of his justice in these acts is probably his reverence for the royal office.

§ 18. *Relations with Tyre* (2 Sam. v. 11) *and their Ethical Consequences.*

David was now king of united Israel. He takes Jerusalem and makes it his capital. Then he builds a palace with the aid of Hiram of Tyre. This commencement of commercial intercourse with foreign Powers is an important event in the history of Hebrew ethics. The people had now settled down to industrial pursuits, and new rights and duties had come into existence. But the entrance into commercial relations with other nations affects ethical conceptions still more deeply. It tends to mitigate the ingrained hostility of race to race which is one of the most powerful habits of savage men, and which survives into less barbarous stages of culture. Trade and commerce create mutual interests between nations, and extend the scope of morals beyond the narrow limits of the individual State. International ethics are impossible until nations have learned that, if they are to take (without war), they must also give. The friendly relations established between David and Tyre were extended by Solomon and his successors.

§ 19. *Jerusalem Made the National Religious Centre* (2 Sam. vi.).

This chapter is one of exceptional interest to the student of Hebrew religion; but it concerns us only in a secondary degree. It is the first stage in the evolution of Hebrew priestism. Hitherto a sacerdotal order had not existed. In the present chapter, for example, it is David himself who leads the worship. He pitches the tent for the ark, he offers burnt offerings and peace offerings before it, he blesses the people in the name of Yahweh, and he distributes the elements of the sacramental feast. There is no other word of priestly service in the narrative from beginning to end. But the establishment of a central sanctuary led the way to the Deuteronomic reform under Josiah, when the provincial high places were abolished, and Jerusalem became the sole religious centre for the Hebrew people. By the time of Josiah (639–608) a priestly order had become differentiated, it had grown enormously in power, and it was able to dictate to the young king the details of his iconoclastic changes. This second centralisation tended still further to the ecclesiastical predominance, and, while it elaborated the cult, it was a doubtful gain to morals. It was the prophets who had preached the higher ethics, the influence of the priest tending rather to formalism and mere religiosity. This is very vividly seen in the glowing utterances of Isaiah (i. 11–17): " To what purpose is the multitude of your sacrifices to me? saith the Lord.......Bring no more vain oblations.......Your new moons and your appointed feasts my soul hateth : they are a trouble to me; I am weary to bear them." Micah is equally explicit (vi. 6–8): "Will the Lord be pleased with thousands of rams, or with ten thousands of rivers of oil?......What doth the Lord require of thee, but to do justly, and to love mercy, and to walk humbly with thy God?" This hostility between the prophets, eager for moral reform, and the priests, zealous for ritual and dogma, is, indeed, a perennial force in the history of thought, culminating every now and then in a religious revolution, under such leaders as Gautama, Jesus Christ, and Mohammed; and, in our own day, breaking out in the utterances of a Carlyle or a Tolstoy, or in the revolt of a sect or party against priestism. This centralisation of the worship of Yahweh would, therefore, seem to have been a retarding influence in ethical development.

The incident of the death of Uzzah (vv. 6–8) calls for a word of comment. It is probably an interpolation of a late date,[1] when the priestly redactor wished to bring the narrative into harmony with the sacerdotalism of his age. He thought it profane for a layman to touch the sacred casket, which, according to the Chronicles (1 Chron. xiii. 2), was in the charge of priests and Levites. To an unpriestly mind, the act of Uzzah would seem to be both reverential and

---

[1] It appears to have been transferred bodily from 1 Chron. xiii. 6–14.

commendable. So, indeed, it appeared to David, who was naturally angry with his god for such unreasonable severity. The ethics of David in this case were higher than those of the priestly editor who ascribed Uzzah's death to divine interposition.

Michal's remonstrance at David's alleged indecency before the ark has an ethical bearing. The king was clothed with a linen ephod, which was probably a loin cloth. According to the Rev. Dr. Moore,[1] "it may perhaps have been" a return to a "primitive custom which antiquity had rendered sacred, as the pilgrims to Mecca to-day must wear the simple loin-cloth, which was once the common dress of the Arabs." It must, however, be remembered that the ancient Canaanitish cults contained elements of gross sensuality, and it is at least possible that David's behaviour represented a partial survival of a ceremonial practice of a very objectionable kind. However this may be, it is evident that the current ethical taste, as represented by Michal, had advanced beyond the coarseness which still lingered in religious ceremony.

§ 20. *Ethics of David's Wars.*

There is nothing in the Biblical narrative to show that David differed from other despots of his time in his treatment of his enemies. We have already seen some examples of his methods before he became king. Royal power did not

---

[1] *Enc. Bib.*, col. 1306.

D

mitigate his severity. When he smote Moab
(2 Sam. viii. 2), he deliberately slew two out of
every three of his conquered foes. His cruelty
to the horses of the king of Zobah is not pleasant
reading (2 Sam. viii. 4). I do not lay stress
upon his treatment of the conquered Ammonites
(2 Sam. xii. 31), as recorded in the English
versions. He is there represented as putting
them under saws, harrows, and axes, and making
them pass through the brick-kiln. The Hebrew
particle translated " under " may quite as fairly
be rendered by " at," and the passage may be a
description of labours forced upon the subject-
people.

§ 21. *David's Kindness to Mephibosheth* (2 Sam. ix.).

It has been suggested that David's behaviour
to the son of his former friend and comrade was
prompted by policy.[1] A more honourable motive
is perhaps equally probable. The king was
endowed with warm emotions, and it is quite
natural that the passion which sometimes blazed
out into ferocity should coexist with strength of
emotion of a gentler kind. Such a combination
is not uncommon in strong natures, especially
among uncultured peoples.

§ 22. *The Uriah Incident* (2 Sam. xi.–xii. 1–25).

We are expressly told (1 Kings xv. 5) that
· "David did that which was right in the eyes of

[1] *Enc. Bib.*, col. 3024.

the Lord, and turned not aside from anything that he commanded him all the days of his life, save only in the matter of Uriah the Hittite." This condemnation is repeatedly expressed in the Biblical narrative. The Chronicler omits the incident, for, when he wrote, the idealizing of David was in progress.

It is important to notice that this censure of David's sins is not based upon their inherent wickedness, but upon their violation of divine command. "Wherefore," we read (xii. 9), " hast thou despised the word of the Lord to do that which is evil in his sight?" And again (ver. 10), " because thou hast despised me, and hast taken the wife of Uriah the Hittite to be thy wife." The conception of moral government suggested by these texts is not an advanced one; but it is far beyond the theology of many barbarians, with whom the adoration of the deity is the supreme consideration, and duty between man and man has no relation to religion at all. Murder and adultery are here regarded as sinful, though they are so regarded because they express contempt of the deity who forbids them. The ethical is subordinated to the theological. The deity is not unmindful of moral distinctions; but he is still " a jealous god," who, if his dignity is touched, may break out upon his contemners as " a consuming fire." This view of ethics will again engage our attention when we come to the numbering of the people.

If Nathan's condemnation of David indicates

that Hebrew theology was not unethical, the punishments inflicted upon him show that the moral standard was still a low one. The penalties threatened (and carried out) are the public seduction of David's wives (xii. 11–12) and the death of Bathsheba's child (ver. 18). The heaviest blows in both examples fall upon the wrong persons. In the latter, a sinless baby dies for an offence of which it knows nothing. In the former, several innocent women are made to suffer public shame and outrage. Could anything be more unjust or more atrocious? What are we to think of the moral standard of a people who can deliberately attribute[1] to their deity the command to perpetrate this manifold and shameless crime? Indeed, the deity is represented as the direct agent. Thus he declares : "I will take thy wives before thine eyes, and give them unto thy neighbour," etc., and "I will do this thing before all Israel, and before the sun." The clumsiness of the operation is equal to its iniquity. It is like the act of a Nihilist who throws a bomb at a despot and misses him, but kills a dozen blameless spectators. The credibility of such an astounding narrative is not, of course, in question here. All that concerns us is the fact that a Hebrew scribe, writing the annals of his nation, believes that this outrage was merely an act of justice by a holy God.

---

[1] These verses (10–12) are assigned by the critics to a Deuteronomic redactor, and, therefore, they date several centuries after David's time. What, then, must have been the standard in his age?

Such ideas of vengeance are, indeed, quite in accordance with the ethics of those barbarous peoples with whom women have no rights, and whose despots are too powerful to suffer the due penalty of their crimes.

The story of the death of the child and the grief of the father is told very pathetically. It seems almost suggested that we ought to sympathize with David in his sorrow. The more advanced ethics of the twentieth century A.D. will not, however, permit us to do this. Our sympathy is rather with the poor infant, with its mother, who had been brought to shame and sin by the unbridled lust of the despotic king, and with Uriah, basely murdered by the sovereign for whom he fought.

A very sinister light is thrown upon David's character by the series of deceptions which led up to the murder, and subsequently sought to hide it. The king devises a cunning scheme (vv. 6–13) to cover his sin with Bathsheba, and to make it appear that Uriah is the father of the child that is to be born. He sends for Uriah, and commands him to go home for rest and refreshment. Uriah refuses to do so on religious grounds. David repeats the manœuvre, and attempts to overcome the scruples of his guest by making him drunk. Again he fails. Uriah definitely refuses to go near his wife. Then the fatal letter to Joab is written. After Uriah's murder there is repeated untruth. David attempts to hoodwink the messenger who brings to him the news of Uriah's death, pretending that it was an ordinary incident in war, "for the sword devoureth one as well as another" (ver. 25).

Bible students have paid little attention to these disgraceful tricks; but it is in such inconspicuous acts of a man's life that his true character is most clearly revealed. Even in the most advanced civilisations, great natures are liable to great crimes; but they do not stoop to the ignoble devices of the trickster. We can make allowances for the murderous fury of Othello: we have nothing but contempt and loathing for the treachery of Iago.

§ 23. *Amnon's Seduction of Tamar* (2 Sam. xiii.).

This picture of human life and passion is full of interest. We see vividly portrayed before us the awakening of Amnon's unholy love; Jonadab's cunning device; the King's daughter (like Homer's princesses) kneading the dough and making cakes for the sham invalid; her unsuspecting innocence; her pitiful appeal to her brother's manliness; Amnon's revulsion of feeling; his brutal expulsion of his injured sister, arrayed in her "garment of divers colours," such as was worn by "the king's daughters that were virgins"; Tamar's pathetic lamentation; Absalom's brotherly comfort; the king's useless anger; Absalom's slow brooding over his revenge; his sudden and unexpected vengeance; the afflicted father lying prostrate on the earth in the depth of his sorrow; the outburst of weeping by the king and his sons; and the flight of Absalom. The narrative bears the impress of naturalness and truth. The personages of the drama behave with the unrestrained emotion characteristic of an uncivilised age. Law is still feeble. The ruler of the State inflicts no penalty upon the guilty Amnon. Either his offence was not then punishable by the law, or the king permitted his fatherly affection to override his sense of right. We are told that he was " very wroth," and that is all.

We see the laxness of David's government of his family not only in his failure to punish Amnon, but also in his omission to call Absalom to account for the assassination of his brother. The king's personal partialities overpower his sense of duty. After the murder, the father's heart goes out more strongly to the murderer than to his victim.

§ 24. *The Woman of Tekoa* (2 Sam. xiv. 2–11).

An interesting ethical question is incidentally introduced in this woman's interview with David. She pretends to appeal to the King's justice against the avenger of blood, who threatens to slay her only remaining son for his brother's manslaughter. Her story is, of course, imaginary, but it as clearly expresses the current ethics of murder as if it were real. The primitive custom of blood-revenge is evidently weakening. The avenger of blood presses for his penalty; but the royal power can intervene. "As the Lord liveth," declares the king, "there shall not one hair of thy son fall to the earth" (ver. 11). It seems to be

admitted that this interposition will thwart the
due course of justice, for the woman says : " My
lord, O king, the iniquity be on me, and on my
father's house : and the king and his throne be
guiltless " (ver. 9). The story affords, however,
a suggestion of better times. Kin-law, often
blind and indiscriminating, is giving place to
royal law, which is a distinct step in advance.
Men infuriated by an injury to one of their
blood are less likely to be just than a ruler, however despotic, unless he is swayed by personal
motives in special cases. David was the first
Israelitish king who commanded a standing
army, and who was thus in some degree raised
above the necessity of relying upon parties or
great families. Under his rule, men could no
longer do that which was right in their own
eyes (Judg. xxi. 25).

§ 25. *Absalom's Outrage upon Joab's Barley* (2 Sam. xiv. 29–33).

Absalom, wishing to secure Joab's intervention with the king, repeatedly sends for him ;
and, when he fails to come, Absalom, as a
reminder, sets fire to Joab's field of barley.
Incidents of this kind throw a flood of light
upon the ethics of the age. The outrage is not
mentioned with any reprobation, and it does not
appear to have been looked upon as anything
very unusual. Joab, of course, remonstrates ;
but he does the bidding of the prince who
employs arson as a persuader. We are reminded
of the playful highwayman who prevailed upon

the coachman to stop by sending a couple of bullets through his head. The methods of the robber and the Hebrew prince were not dissimilar.

§ 26. *David's Behaviour to Ittai the Gittite* (2 Sam. xv. 18–22).

Absalom's rebellion has broken out, and David is fleeing from Jerusalem. His bodyguard of foreigners includes 600 men from Gath under Ittai, who accompanies the king in his flight. David orders him to return, whether to his own home in Gath or to Absalom in Jerusalem is not clear. Ittai had not long before entered the king's service, and his master tells him that, having come to him so recently, he was under no obligation to render aid in this time of exile and danger. This appears to be very magnanimous, and perhaps was really so. But why should David have been so careful of the safety of a Philistine mercenary? It is difficult not to suspect a little idealism here.

§ 27. *The Cursing of Shimei* (2 Sam. xvi. 5–14).

Again we seem driven to suspect an idealizing touch. That David, surrounded by his warriors, should tolerate the insults of Shimei, and meekly ascribe his curses to divine command, is scarcely credible. There is improbability, too, in the alleged conduct of Shimei. The king, we are told, had "all the people and all the mighty men on his right hand and on his left." Is it likely that one man would dare to rail and

throw stones at a warlike monarch in the midst
of his army? Such behaviour could be only
described as insane. It seems more probable
that the incident arose out of the desire of the
writer to paint David's character in exceptionally
bright colours. We are reminded by it of the
description in the Deutero-Isaiah, where the
Jewish people are idealized as the Suffering Saint
of Yahweh :—

"I gave my back to the smiters, and my
cheeks to them that plucked off the hair: I hid
not my face from shame and spitting" (Isa. l. 6).

And again :—

"He was despised, and rejected of men; a
man of sorrows, and acquainted with grief"
(liii. 3).

Such meekness hardly consists with the
character of the vindictive warrior who threatened
a bloody vengeance for Nabal's churlishness, and
inflicted heavy penalties for the insults of the
children of Ammon. I do not, therefore, feel at
liberty to use this incident as indicating a phase
of David's true nature.

§ 28. *David's Lament over Absalom* (xviii. 33).

There would seem to be no reason to doubt the
substantial accuracy of the narrative of Absalom's
revolt and its failure. The rebellion itself and
its main incidents are events that might have
occurred in any Semitic state of that period.
The king's solicitude for the safety of his ungrateful son, and his extravagant grief at his
death, are the natural outcome of an energetic

and impulsive nature. David's loves and his hates give us the impression of a highly emotional character, prone to extremes of either good or evil. His warm natural affections have done much in popular esteem to extenuate his moral defects.

§ 29. *Hushai's Counter-treachery* (2 Sam. xv. 32–37, xvi. 16–19, xvii. 5–15).

Hushai, with David's consent, enters Absalom's service as David's spy, to mislead the prince by bad counsel, and betray him to the king. Such conduct is certainly not in accordance with a high moral standard. Absalom was basely ungrateful to a kind and indulgent father; but it is not lawful to fight wicked men with the weapons of wickedness. There is no evidence, however, to show that Hushai's behaviour was censured by the age in which his treachery was described. Certainly, David approved of it, and did not scruple to profit by it.

§ 30. *David's Treatment of his Concubines* (xx. 3).

By the advice of Ahithophel, Absalom had publicly seduced ten of the king's concubines. This probably is the punishment threatened by Nathan (2 Sam. xii. 11) for David's sin with Bathsheba; for, though Nathan speaks of wives, the distinction in that age between wives and concubines was not a wide one. On Absalom's part, this offence against morals was an act of policy. According to a barbarous Semitic custom, the successor to the throne took over the wives and concubines of the last king as a part of his personal property. David himself had done this (2 Sam. xii. 8). The seduction of his father's concubines implied that Absalom had assumed the crown and cut off the possibility of retreat. On the suppression of the rebellion, when David returned to his capital, he commanded the imprisonment of the unfortunate women, and they were "shut up to the day of their death, living in widowhood."

The punishment of these concubines proves that, in his treatment of women, David was not in advance of his age. Their offence against morals was entirely involuntary. They had no more choice in the matter than if they had been cows or sheep. To punish them was an offence against equity. Both Absalom and his father behaved with the brutal contempt for the rights of women characteristic of a barbarous age.

§ 31. *Gratitude to Barzillai* (2 Sam. xvii. 27–29, xix. 31–39).

The reward which David offers for Barzillai's services in the time of the king's flight and adversity was liberal, and evinced a generous nature. In the virtue of gratitude the Hebrew monarch was superior to some modern potentates, such as our Charles II., who, after the Restoration, treated with callous neglect most of the Cavaliers who had sacrificed their wealth and their blood in his cause.

§ 32. *The Vengeance of the Gibeonites* (2 Sam. xxi. 1–14).

Several interesting questions are suggested by these verses. The following most nearly relate to our inquiry :—

(1) THE ETHICAL CONCEPTIONS FORMED OF YAHWEH BY THE WRITER OF THE NARRATIVE.

There is a three years' famine, and we are told (ver. 1) that it was a punishment for Saul's cruelty to the Gibeonites. But why should the penalty have been inflicted so long after the perpetration of the crime that the sufferers could see no connection between the two events until they were informed of it by an oracle? Why, too, should Saul's fault have been visited upon the whole people? Such a substitution of the innocent for the guilty was surely not calculated to create among the Hebrews a high conception of Divine justice. It stands, indeed, upon the same ethical plane as the pestilence sent by Apollo upon the Greeks because their king had insulted his priest.[1]

Yet even the three years' famine does not satisfy the demands of divine justice for Saul's crime. Yahweh is not placated until he sees the even descendants of the offender hanging before him (ver. 9) in the mountain. " After that," we are informed (ver. 14), " God was intreated for the land."

This strange description of an alleged divine procedure is gravely placed before us by a writer

---

[1] *Iliad*, A, 10 *et seq.*

who was, doubtless, zealous for the honour of the God of Israel.

(2) THE ETHICS OF THE GIBEONITES.

Their demand for vengeance was quite in accord with current ideas. The vendetta, as we have seen, had not yet been superseded by royal law. The Gibeonites appeal to the king himself for the surrender of Saul's descendants, and their vengeance is deemed so righteous that it is carried out in the very presence of the deity, who approves the deed.

(3) THE ETHICS OF DAVID.

If the Biblical narrative is correct, David's surrender was a violation of a solemn oath (§ 10, p. 25). Yet David spares Mephibosheth, the son of Jonathan, " because of the Lord's oath that was sworn between them " (2 Sam. xxi. 7). Why he should keep his oath in one case and break it in others is not very intelligible. Is it that he was personally friendly to Mephibosheth and indifferent to the rest? If so, we cannot form a high opinion of his impartiality as supreme judge of the realm. Putting the apparent perjury on one side, we find that David acquiesces i the barbarous custom of blood-revenge. He sacrifices the lives of seven innocent men to preserve the favour of his deity.

The obscurity investing this account will perhaps be removed if we can accept the suggestion that the Gibeonites, murdered by Saul, were the priests of Yahweh, who had succoured David when he fled to them at Nob

(1 Sam. xxii. 18).   It has been contended[1] that the name " Nob " is corrupt, and that " Gibeon " is meant. Gibeon was " the great high place " (1 Kings iii. 4) where Solomon made his stupendous sacrifice of a thousand burnt offerings. It is implied, in the passage before us, that the slaughter of the Gibeonites was a well-known event ; but we know absolutely nothing about it, unless it is the massacre at Nob, which must have become notorious.

If this identification be accepted, the reason why the crime was deemed so flagrant becomes apparent.   The murdered men were priests. The narrative before us is interpolated in the general history subsequent to the separation made between the Books of Samuel and the Books of Kings, and is several centuries later than J, when the priestly spirit had grown much stronger. Whether it belongs to the time of the Exile, and is a part of the Priestly Code (P), is not certain ; but it is in the same vein of thought, and ranks offences against the cult and its priests as of supreme heinousness.   It would, therefore, appear that low ethical standards were in force even as late as the Captivity, so far at least as the priesthood was concerned. The moral sense must indeed have been extremely immature, or strangely perverted, when it could attribute to the God of Israel acts of such rank injustice. Yet perhaps even these crude conceptions were a moral advance, inasmuch as they were ethical

[1] *Enc. Bib.*, col. 3430.

at all.   In early times, it may be even in David's
age, deities were not regarded as endowed with
moral qualities.

§ 33. *The Song of Triumph and the Last Words* (2 Sam. xxii.–xxiii. 7).

The song is in substance Psa. xviii., and is
much later than the time of David.   The thought
is far in advance of his age, the ethical ideas
being in line with the Deuteronomic teaching.   The theology is monotheistic, and God is ✓
depicted as a moral judge and ruler, who raises
the humble and abases the proud.   The judgments and statutes of God are the rule of life.
His way is perfect, and his word is tried.   Such
conceptions are inconceivable as existing in a
pre-prophetic age.

A comparison with the "Song of Moses"
(Deut. xxxii.) points in the same direction.   The
mode of thought is similar.   It is not improbable
that they are by the same writer.   The peculiar
description of God as a "Rock" occurs six times
in the "Song of Moses," and six times in the
Song of Triumph and the Last Words.   Elsewhere in the Old Testament it is found only in
the Psalms (several times), twice in Isaiah, and
once in the Song of Hannah.   The similarity of
thought is also seen in the comparison of a few
passages.   Compare "For their Rock is not as
our Rock" (Deut. xxxii. 31) with "For who is
God save the Lord, and who is a Rock save our
God?" (2 Sam. xxii. 32); and "The Rock, his
work is perfect; For all his ways are judgment"

(Deut. xxxii. 4) with "As for God, his way is perfect: The word of the Lord is tried" (2 Sam. xxii. 31). But the two chapters should be compared in detail. Now, if the "Song of Moses" is by the same author as the Song of Triumph and the Last Words, it is obvious that we cannot rely upon the authorship alleged by the Biblical writers, and we must be guided solely by the internal evidence.

A comparison between the Song of Triumph and the Lament over Saul and Jonathan is fatal to a Davidic origin for at least one of them. The Lament is absolutely unethical and untheological; the Song is saturated with theology and morals. The former is pure humanism; the latter is full of supernatural interventions. The Lament is exquisitely pathetic; the Song is distinguished rather for sublimity and vigour.

We may safely conclude that the Song and the Last Words are not the work of David, and therefore they throw no light upon his moral character. They express the ideas which a writer living several centuries later than David believed could be appropriately put into the mouth of the national hero.

§ 34. *The Numbering of the People* (2 Sam. xxiv.).

This account is perplexing in the extreme. It is difficult for a modern moralist to put himself in the place of a writer who describes his deity as punishing for an offence which he had himself commanded. Yet this is the plain meaning of the words (ver. 1): "And again the

anger of the Lord was kindled against Israel, and
he moved David against them, saying, Go,
number Israel and Judah." David obeys the
order, and his obedience is punished by the
death of 70,000 of his subjects. In analyzing
this narrative, it will be desirable to proceed
(a) on the basis of the traditional view of the
chronological relations of the books of the Old
Testament, and (b) in the light of the results
obtained by modern criticism.

(a) On the traditional view, David's census is
a violation of a Mosaic law. He numbers the
people "without requiring the statutable offering
of half a shekel a head."[1] The statute here
mentioned is in Exod. xxx. 11–16: "When
thou takest the sum of the children of Israel,
according to those that are numbered of them,
then shall they give every man a ransom for his
soul unto the Lord, when thou numberest them;
that there be no plague among them, when thou
numberest them." The plague is thus distinctly
threatened by implication if the ransom is not
paid. In ver. 13 the ransom is fixed at half a
shekel. In Exod. xxxviii. 25, 26, we read that
the tax was actually levied, and amounted to
100 talents and 1,775 shekels. Censuses are
recorded at which no ransom-money is mentioned. One of these is made by Moses (Numb.
xxvi.), and one by Saul (1 Sam. xv. 4); yet there
is no suggestion in either case that a sin has
been committed. If David had the Exodus-law

[1] Smith's *Dict. Bible*, Census:

before him, it is strange that he should have broken it, and it is equally strange that in the account in 2 Sam. xxiv. no reference is made to the ransom. On the traditional hypothesis, however, we are bound to believe that the census was an offence against divine law.

The following points are stated in, or are fair inferences from, the narrative :—

(1) That in the age succeeding David it was believed that God[1] punished men for an act which he had himself commanded.

(2) That the punishment was inflicted, not upon the guilty David, but upon his innocent people.

(3) That when the census was finished David was sorry for what he had done.

(4) That as a penalty he was offered (a) seven years' famine, or (b) three months' flight before his enemies, or (c) three days' pestilence.

(5) That David piously leaves himself in the hands of God, and thus escapes the punishment of his offence. Equity would have said that the sinner should himself bear the suffering, and thus the three months' flight before his enemies was the choice he ought to have made. Three months' inconvenience, and perhaps pain, to himself would have saved the lives of 70,000 guiltless persons, his own subjects. Honest men do not understand the piety of a king who transfers to others the penalty of his own fault.

---

[1] In this place I purposely avoid reference to the parallel account in 1 Chron. xxi.

(6) That David himself recognises the injustice of the punishment inflicted by his God. "But these sheep," he pathetically pleads, "what have they done? Let thine hand, I pray thee, be against me, and against my father's house." This belated repentance appears to have been fruitless. We do not read that either David or any of his "father's house" suffered for this sin.

This narrative represents the Deity as unjust and cruel; it represents David as foolish, selfish, and cowardly. The conceptions of both David and his God are the natural products of a barbarous and unenlightened age. The man may well have been "after the heart" of a Deity whose character was reflected in himself.

(b) In the light of the results obtained by modern criticism, the following considerations suggest themselves:—

The Exodus-law which David is supposed to have violated is a part of the Priestly Code (P). This view is now generally accepted; but see Canon Driver[1] and the *Encyclopædia Biblica*.[2] The Priestly Code was published by Ezra after the Exile—that is, about 500 years after the time of David, who, of course, could have known nothing of the law which he is alleged to have broken. We are, therefore, in the dark as to the nature of David's sin. We can hardly accept the improbable suggestion that it consisted in the pride of his heart at the magnitude

---

[1] *Intro. Lit. O. Test.*, 34.   [2] Col. 1449.

of his kingdom. I say "improbable," because it is quite out of harmony with the principles of ethical evolution that so refined a sin should have been deemed worthy of severe punishment in the age of David. Pride was so common and natural an emotion in the mind of a semi-civilised Eastern despot that the dreadful judgments inflicted upon David's people would have been grotesque in their inappropriateness.

Another explanation regards the numbering of the people as preliminary to an attack upon the national liberties. But what were these liberties? The government was a pure despotism, "tempered by assassination." There was no parliament to be crushed, or national franchise to be abrogated. The crown was not yet hereditary; but its powers were not limited by constitutional restraints. Even if there were liberties to be destroyed, how would the death by plague of 70,000 of the assertors of those liberties help to preserve them?

An examination of the narrative raises grave doubts of its reliability. The result of the census, not including Levi and Benjamin, was a total of 1,300,000 fighting men, which the Chronicler raises to 1,570,000. Even on the lower estimate the total population could not be less than 3,000,000. Yet the dominions of David did not greatly exceed 6,000 square miles, or about the size of Yorkshire. That county, in the census of 1891, contained a little over 3,000,000 people, a large proportion of whom are concentrated in large manufacturing towns. It is improbable that the Palestine of David, being without important manufactures, and cultivated by antique and imperfect methods, could have maintained more than one-third of that number, which would be rather more than the population of Yorkshire in 1801. The numbers given in the census of David must, therefore, be imaginary. Another improbability is in the time consumed in taking the census. We are told that it occupied nine months and twenty days! The thing is incredible.

It is not easy to determine why the priestly redactor inserted this account in the chronicle of David's reign. We may suggest with some probability that a reason had to be given for the selection of Jerusalem as the site of the new central sanctuary. The place for the new altar was to be distinguished by a great manifestation of divine power. The arrest of the pestilence was the critical event, and the altar was erected on the spot where the destroying angel sheathed his sword (1 Chron. xxi. 27). Then a cause for the plague had to be invented.

Whether or not the Biblical account of the numbering of the people be accepted as true to fact is not essential to my purpose. At the very least it shows us that a pious Hebrew writer, living in a more advanced phase of ethical development than David's, describes his Deity and his ideal royal saint as failing to rise above even a low standard of morals.

§ 35. *David's Dying Instructions* (1 Kings ii. 1–10).

The last words of the aged warrior are of a piece with his life. They breathe the old spirit of mingled ferocity and kindness, associated with the lack of moral courage, which so often weakened his sense of justice. Joab is to be put to death for his assassination of Abner and Amasa. Barzillai is to be rewarded and cherished for his services to David during his flight from Absalom. The insults of Shimei are to be avenged by a bloody death. But why is the odium of the acts of vengeance to be shifted to the shoulders of Solomon? Why had not David himself, as the upholder of national justice, called Joab to account for his crimes? Was it policy or timidity that winked at the offences of the useful and influential general? The King was bound by oath not to punish Shimei, but he was under no such obligation to Joab. He had condoned his officer's crimes, and had been rewarded by years of faithful and successful service. The claims of equity would surely have been met by a less sanguinary penalty.

The punishment of Shimei also does not commend itself to modern ideas of justice. David had sworn that the railer should not die for his offence. To hand him over to another for the death penalty is an evasion of his oath which closely approaches perjury.

Thus ended David, urging revenge for the insults of Shimei with his dying breath. It was the death of a barbarian warrior and chieftain, with a conscience dim and half-developed, human alike in its promptings to generous deeds and its facile yielding to selfish passions. It was not the death of a saint, scarcely that of a righteous man, judged even by the ethical standards of the most backward of modern civilisations.

SUMMARY OF THE DETAILS OF DAVID'S CHARACTER

WE are now in a position to summarise the preceding evidence, and to form an impartial, if imperfect, conception of David's character. It will be convenient to look at each side of it separately.

§ 1. *Favourable Features.*

The glowing colours in which former ages have depicted the moral nature of the hero-king have not been entirely false. Large-hearted men must needs win affection, and affection covers a multitude of sins, especially when the sinner wears a royal crown. David was gifted with strong emotions. His love for the ungrateful Absalom, his tender friendship for Jonathan, his gratitude to Barzillai, are very pleasing features. His love to Jonathan descends to Mephibosheth ; he forgives and cherishes the son for the father's sake. We cannot but admire his loyalty to Saul, though it was partly compounded of selfish elements. He saves the life of his sleeping enemy, he utters a noble eulogy over his death, he inflicts capital punishment upon the Amalekite who boasts himself the slayer of Saul, and upon the assassins of Ishbosheth,

Saul's son and successor. His magnanimity
to Ittai, the Philistine mercenary, seems to be
a generous sentiment. David was not without
a sense of equity, as seen in his division of the
spoil recovered at Ziglag between the actual
fighters and their comrades who had been
precluded from joining them. His sense of
justice seems indeed to have risen higher than
that which was afterwards assigned to his Deity.
"These sheep, what have they done?" is his
pathetic appeal against the misdirected vengeance
of Heaven.

§ 2. *Unfavourable Features.*

The other side of David's character presents
many unpleasing features. Indeed, a careful
analysis of the narrative brings to light defects
for which I was scarcely prepared. So much
emphasis has been laid in Scripture upon David's
sins in the matter of Uriah and Bathsheba[1] that
the impression has widely prevailed that the rest
of his life was comparatively blameless. The
testimony of the Bible is most explicit. "David
did that which was right in the eyes of the Lord,
and turned not aside from anything that he commanded him all the days of his life, save only in
the matter of Uriah the Hittite" (1 Kings xv. 5).
We are thus driven to conclude either that the
standard of morals current under the monarchy
was very low, or that the writer was grievously

[1] The recent attempt of Dieulafoy (*David the King*, 211–264)
to whitewash David at the expense of Bathsheba receives little
support from the Biblical story.

mistaken. Our investigation has shown that David's character was seriously defective.

One of the most unexpected results of my inquiry is the revelation of David's *untruthfulness*. I have called attention to the false excuses sent through Jonathan to Saul; to the lying representation made by David to Ahimelech, whereby he secured the aid of the priest, and involved him and his kin in the sanguinary penalties of treason; to the unseemly exhibition of sham madness before Achish; to the lies told to Achish over the Geshurite raid; to David's subsequent repetition of his untruth to Achish in the seemingly innocent inquiry, "What have I done?"; to his condonation of the treachery of Hushai; and to the violation of his oath to Saul. But perhaps the most repulsive of David's unveracities were the contemptible tricks by which he tried to cloak his sin with Bathsheba. All of these deceptions, some of them resulting in calamities to numbers of innocent people, are described in the Biblical narrative without the slightest hint of censure, and we are led to suspect that the Hebrews of the age succeeding David did not regard deceit as immoral. We find, in truth, that, even in later times, Micaiah, a prophet of Yahweh, sets forth the Deity as putting a lying spirit in the mouth of certain prophets (1 Kings xxi. 20–23). Now, if a prophet of the reign of Ahab can be represented by a writer living some centuries later as attributing mendacity to his God, it is clear that such unveracity was not considered sinful even in that later time. David's deceits were, therefore, the natural outcome of the age in which he lived.

Allied to David's untruthfulness is his *defective sense of justice*. He punishes the ten concubines for an offence in which they were more sinned against than sinning, while his surrender of the seven descendants of Saul to the vengeance of the Gibeonites indicates that he had not risen above the rank injustice of the vendetta. His choice of the three days' plague instead of a penalty falling upon himself was a glaring act of injustice.

David's *lack of moral courage* is very manifest. His selection of the three days' plague, his transference to Solomon of the responsibility for the punishment of Joab, and his neglect to punish his sons, Amnon and Absalom, for serious crimes, are cases in point.

The *cruelty* and *ferocity* of David place him on a level with the barbarous kings of surrounding heathendom. We may recall his Geshurite raid, when he spared not woman or child " lest they should tell on him," his houghing of the horses of the King of Zobah, his slaughter of two-thirds of his Moabite prisoners, and his contemplated vengeance on Nabal and his following. His purchase of his wife Michal by the slaughter of a hundred (or two hundred ?) Philistines may, perhaps, be defended as an act of legitimate war; but the mutilation of his slaughtered enemies, though in accordance with the usage of his age, is revolting to the modern conscience.

Of David's *sensuality*, of his numerous wives

and concubines, of the Abishag incident, and of Bathsheba, we need not speak. He was probably no worse than the average king of his time. Of the murder of Uriah enough has been said by other writers.

The above facts are narrated in the Bible, not by enemies, but by admirers and friends, probably by Judæan scribes of the centuries succeeding David. We may fairly assume that, though they strove to write true history, they were not unbiassed in their judgment. If, then, such be the picture drawn by the hands of admiring friends, it is reasonable to conjecture that the ruthless impartiality of a Tacitus would have presented to posterity a David of less attractive qualities than the David I have here extracted from the older Biblical records.

§ 3. *David's Ethics Further Illustrated by his Conception of his Deity.*

The morals of the gods of a nation are a measure of the current ethical ideals. The gods of Homer are magnified men, with the virtues and vices of the Greeks of his age. As Greek theology developed, it grew more and more ethical. Men like Socrates neglected their fathers' deities, and recognised a supreme god with high moral qualities. This moralised deity was the creation of a moralised people, or rather a moralised thinking class, for the ignorant masses have always clung to the cruder theological conceptions of their ancestors, and lagged behind the thinkers. David, we may justly suppose, as one of the choicer minds of his age, would be rather in advance of it than behind it, and his ideal of Deity would probably approach the highest ethics which had been attained in a people who had not yet produced its thinkers. What, then, were his thoughts of Yahweh, his national God?

There are indications that the theology attributed to David in the Bible combined gross and primitive ideas with the ethical conceptions of a more advanced age. The earlier and non-ethical stage of thought appears in a very instructive passage (1 Sam. xxvi. 19): "If it be the Lord that hath stirred thee up against me, let him accept (*Heb.*, smell) an offering." Here David conceives it possible that his God should be the author of Saul's malignant designs against himself, and he suggests that the Deity's anger should be placated by the smell of a burnt offering. Both of these ideas belong to barbarian, almost savage, thought. The god of the early theologian is a strong, passionate, selfish despot, jealous for his own glory, and regardless of human interests. As Tylor writes:[1] "The moral element is little represented in the religion of the lower races." Ellis,[2] describing certain peoples on the Gold Coast, remarks: "The most atrocious crimes committed as between man and man the gods can view with equanimity. These are man's concern, and must be rectified or punished by

---

[1] *Prim. Cult.*, 3rd ed. 1891, I. 427.
[2] Quoted in Spencer's *Principles of Ethics*, 309.

man." That such ideas as these survived into a more advanced stage of culture is very clearly seen in Homer. Jealousy, revenge, deceit, and lust are prominent characteristics of the immortal gods. They "delude men with false appearances; even combine, as Zeus and Athene did, to prompt the breaking of treaties solemnly sworn to."[1] This indifference to right and wrong is equally apparent in the supposition that Yahweh inspired Saul's evil designs against David.

David's suggested remedy for the mischief is also in strict accordance with the practice of ancient paganism. An offering to placate a hostile god is one of the most common of barbarian rites. It is found in all parts of the world. Tylor gives numerous examples. The negroes of Labode hand in bottles of brandy to the residence of their god, Jimawong, and fancy that he drinks it, and is pleased. The Ostyaks "used to leave a horn of snuff for their god." The incense of tobacco, with the invocation, "Smoke, Sun," is offered to that luminary by the Sioux. The Zulus burn the fat of the caul with incense "to give the spirits a sweet savour." Similar practices are found in association with a much higher culture. When Odysseus enters Hades, he propitiates[2] the spirits by a bloody offering:—

"Now the wan shades we hail, th' infernal gods,
    To speed our course, and waft us o'er the flood:

[1] Spencer's *Data of Sociology* (1893), 193.
[2] Pope's *Odyssey*, xi. 35–38.

> So shall a barren heifer from the stall
> Beneath the knife upon your altars fall."

Sometimes the sacrifice is burnt. "A savour of burnt offerings went up in wreathing smoke to heaven."[1] In Semitic lore, burnt offerings are represented as pleasing to the senses of deity. The Babylonian deluge-legend narrates that when, on the subsidence of the waters, a burnt sacrifice was offered,

> "The gods smelled the odour, the gods smelled the sweet odour."

So, too, in the Hebrew account it is related (Gen. viii. 21) that "the Lord smelled the sweet savour." The Levitical law, describing the various kinds of sacrifices, frequently repeats the formula: "It is an offering made by fire, of a sweet savour into the Lord."

David's own practices were in accordance wit primitive beliefs. When he brings up the ark, itself the evidence of a very crude theology, he offers sacrifices and dances before it, wearing a linen ephod. He repeatedly consults the oracle of Yahweh when going into battle or undertaking important affairs; just as the ancient Greeks appealed to the oracle of Apollo at Delphi, and Roman augurs sought the will of the gods in the entrails of animals. If we accept 1 Sam. xvii. as authentic history, we learn that David regarded his deity as a war-god. Yahweh is "the God of the armies of Israel"; and, again, "the battle is the Lord's." This low conception of deity is,

---

[1] *Iliad*, i. 317.

of course, very widely spread. Homeric gods join in the battles of mortals, Admiral Togo informs the Mikado that his great victory over the Russians was "due to the brilliant virtue of your Majesty and the protection of the spirits of your Imperial ancestors," and English Christians pray to the All-merciful to fight on their side, to " scatter our enemies and make them fall."

Associated with the theological beliefs of savage peoples, David appears to have held somewhat higher views of the character of his deity. The evidence, indeed, is not very decisive. The Judaic document affords but one passage in which David rises to faith in Yahweh as a moral being. It occurs in the very interview with Saul in which David utters such different sentiments. He declares (ver. 23) that " the Lord shall render to every man his righteousness and his faithfulness: forasmuch as the Lord delivered thee into my hand to-day, and I would not put forth my hand against the Lord's anointed." Here Yahweh is represented as recognising the merit of righteous conduct. Then David goes on to apply this principle to himself. " And, behold, as thy life was much set by this day in mine eyes, so let my life be much set by in the eyes of the Lord, and let him deliver me out of all tribulation." The two views seem scarcely consistent with each other. If Yahweh has so little regard for David's innocence that he might conceivably stir up Saul's malignity against him, why should he be thought likely to reward David's generosity to Saul with deliverance from tribulation? David appears to dimly apprehend a moral character in his deity; but he has not risen above the primitive belief that a god is the author of both good and evil.

The Elohist puts into David's mouth words expressive of a still more advanced conception of Yahweh. They occur in the Nabal narrative (1 Sam. xxv.). David, in his anger at Nabal's churlishness, gives order for the slaughter of all his male connections (ver. 22). Abigail apologizes for her husband, and pleads with David for mercy, remarking that "the Lord hath withholden thee from bloodguiltiness and from avenging thyself with thy hand" (ver. 26). David accepts the apology. Nabal then conveniently dies, apparently as a judgment upon him for his stinginess. When David heard of this event, he said (ver. 39): "Blessed be the Lord, that hath pleaded the cause of my reproach from the hand of Nabal, and hath kept back his servant from evil: and the evil-doing of Nabal hath the Lord returned upon his own head." In these words there is a clearer perception of ethical judgment. Yahweh restrains David from evil, and punishes Nabal for his ingratitude.

I find some difficulty in accepting the historical accuracy of this account. Abigail's speech to David (vv. 26–31) reads like the disquisition of a theologian. Her metaphors are not the natural expression of a woman pleading for mercy, and her definite prophecy of David's accession to the kingdom has a suspicious ring. The judgment which falls so suddenly upon Nabal must also be regarded as indicating a later stage of thought, approaching the Deuteronomic habit of ascribing moral causes to events.

After forming this opinion, I consulted the *Encyclopædia Biblica*, and found that Canon Cheyne describes[1] the story of Nabal as a " legend." However this may be, we may safely accept the narrative as expressing the moral conceptions of an age later than David's, and, therefore, of no use for the purpose of this section.

In 2 Sam. vii. David offers a long prayer to Yahweh, but he does not attribute to his deity any moral qualities, except that his " words are truth." Yet the chapter is admitted to be later than J. For the same reason 2 Sam. xxi.–xxiv. cannot be used here.

Our analysis has thus reduced David's ascription of a moral character to his deity to the one passage (1 Sam. xxvi. 23, 24).

The suggestion that David combined ethical views of Yahweh with a more primitive form of thought receives some confirmation from what we have learned from other sources of the evolution of theology. At first, gods have no moral character. Then they become ethical, and are good or bad, or a mixture of the two. But men's thoughts about them remain confused and inconsistent. We see this very clearly in the poems of Homer. The immortals are sometimes the

---

[1] Col. 3253.

mere causes of natural phenomena. Storms arise because Poseidon hurls his "forky trident," and earthquakes are caused by the nod of Zeus. But they are also moral agents, generally bad or dubious. A higher ethic here and there emerges. We read that "God looks upon the children of men, and punishes the wrongdoer." And, again: "The gods love not violence and wrong, but the man whose ways are righteous, him they honour."[1] It is interesting to note that Homer is believed to have lived about 850 B.C., so that his poems are probably contemporaneous with the writings of the J-redactor. The parallelism of thought between the two writers, Hebrew and Greek, is very instructive.

We conclude that, as David's conception of the moral character of his deity was a low one, his own ideal of conduct was also low.

---

[1] These quotations are from Froude's *Short Studies*, Homer.

PART III.

THE IDEAL DAVID

The foregoing evidence has brought before us a very different David from the devout, spiritually-minded saint of ecclesiastical tradition. But it is the evidence of the most trustworthy portion of the Bible record. It is obvious that writers of later epochs were less likely to be accurately informed, and more prone to be influenced by the mythopœic spirit. David, as the creator of the united monarchy, made a vivid impression on the imagination of the Hebrew people, and his figure grew in impressiveness and majesty as it was viewed through the deepening mist of successive centuries. He was the instrument by whom the national deity had raised his people to the highest point of their glory, and he came to be regarded as Yahweh's chosen one, his "anointed" in a very special sense. Thus, as the Hebrew religion grew more pure and moral, the spiritual and ethical qualities of later ages tended to accrete round the form of the nation's hero-king. Virtues are ascribed to him which probably did not exist in Israel until several centuries after his death. The fierce, vindictive soldier softens into a meek forgiver of injuries;

the cunning trickster shines forth the embodi-
ment of heavenly truth ; and, in the partial pages
of the priestly Chronicler, even the notorious
Uriah murder entirely disappears. It will now
be our task to trace the process which created
the ideal David. We shall examine the testimony of the Bible, taking the books, as nearly
as possible, in the order of time.

DIVISION 1.—THE GROWTH OF THE IDEAL.

Amos (765–750 B.C.).

Amos is the earliest of all the extant Hebrew
writers who succeeded the historians of David's
life. The Books of the Chronicles of the Kings
of Israel and Judah, referred to so frequently in
the Books of Kings, are lost. Probably no part
of the Books of Kings (except 1 Kings i., ii.) was
written before the reign of Josiah (*circ*. 637–
608 B.C.). Any references to David made by the
prophet Amos would, therefore, be of much
interest.

David is mentioned twice in the Book of Amos.
The first notice is in vi. 5 : "That devise for
themselves instruments of music, like David"
(*marg.* "David's "). This sentence occurs in a
passage descriptive of the luxurious nobles of
Samaria. Robertson Smith[1] classes David himself with these. He writes that Amos "represents David as the chosen model of the *dilettanti*
nobles of Ephraim, who lay stretched on beds

[1] *The Old Testament in the Jewish Church*, p. 205.

of ivory, etc." If this interpretation could be accepted, it would seem to prove that the idealizing process had not yet begun; but it cannot be accepted. "Like David," or "David's," apparently refers only to the clause "that devise for themselves instruments of music," and is almost certainly a gloss by a later writer desirous of indicating that the instruments were such as David used. The passage has, therefore, no ethical bearing.

The second reference is in ix. 11: "In that day will I raise up the tabernacle of David that is fallen, etc." This passage, and the continuation to the end of the chapter, is clearly an addition of Exilic or post-Exilic age. The "tabernacle of David" could not be said to have fallen until the overthrow of the Judæan kingdom in the year 586 B.C. "And I will bring again the captivity of my people Israel" (ver. 14) is obviously later than the fall of Samaria in 722 B.C., and therefore after the time of Amos. We must, I think, conclude that Amos did not refer to David at all. This, perhaps, need not surprise us when we reflect that Amos, a Judæan, was preaching to the people of Israel, who could have had little enthusiasm for the house of David, from which they had revolted.

Hosea (740–720 B.C.).

The only reference to David in this prophet is in iii. 5: "Afterwards shall the children of Israel return, and seek the Lord their God, and David their king; and shall come with fear unto

the Lord and to his goodness in the latter days."
This passage refers to a " return," and implies ✗
the Exile. It must, therefore, be regarded as a
late interpolation.

Isaiah (740–700 B.C.).

The following passages refer to David :—

ix. 7. " Of the increase of his government and
of peace there shall be no end upon the throne
of David, and upon his kingdom, to establish it,
and to uphold it with judgement and with
righteousness from henceforth even for ever."
This is part of a Messianic prophecy (ix. 1–7).
The opinion of critics is strongly in favour of its ✗
post-Exilic date.

xi. 1. "And there shall come forth a shoot
out of the stock of Jesse."

xi. 10. "And it shall come to pass in that day
that the root of Jesse, which standeth for an
ensign of the people, unto him shall the nations
seek."

The eleventh chapter is in the style of the
Exilic or post-Exilic writers, and the latter part
refers to a return from exile for both Judah and
Israel. It is certainly later than Isaiah.

xvi. 5. " And a throne shall be established in
mercy, and one shall sit thereon in truth, in the
tent of David, judging and seeking judgement,
and swift to do righteousness."

This verse is an interpolation in the middle of
a prophecy against Moab. Its position is forced,
and its style late.

xxxvii. 35. " For I will defend this city to

save it, for mine own sake, and for my servant David's sake."

This is considered by Cheyne, our highest authority on Isaiah, to be post-Exilic.

xxxviii. 5. " Go, and say unto Hezekiah, Thus saith the Lord, the God of David thy father, I have heard thy prayer, I have seen thy tears."

This verse is probably post-Isaian; but, in any case, it has no value for our purpose.

lv. 3. " I will make an everlasting covenant with you, even the sure mercies of David."

It is generally admitted that this passage is Exilic or post-Exilic.

The conclusions here summarised are not all to be accepted as absolutely certain; but they represent the results of the ripest criticism, and they at least render it unsafe to base upon the passages in question the belief that Isaiah wrote anything about David.

Jeremiah (627–588 B.C.).

I have collected fourteen references to David in this book. Of these, the following may be thought to have ethical signification :—

xxiii. 5. " Behold the days come, saith the Lord, that I will raise unto David a righteous Branch, and he shall reign as king and deal wisely, and shall execute judgement and justice in the land."

This is regarded by Professor Schmidt as a very late interpolation.

xxxiii. 15, 17, 21, 26. " In those days, and at that time, will I cause a Branch of righteousness to grow up unto David, and he shall execute judgement and righteousness in the land."...... "For thus saith the Lord: David shall never want a man to sit upon the throne of the house of Israel.".....". "Then may also my covenant be broken with David my servant, that he should not have a son to reign upon his throne."...... "Then will I cast away the seed of Jacob, and of David my servant."

The passage (vv. 14–26) containing these extracts does not occur in the Septuagint, and is quite generally rejected.

There remain ten non-ethical Davidic references. They merely allude to kings "sitting on the throne of David," to the "house of David," or similar expressions. Yet most of these do not belong to Jeremiah's prophecies. Some of them are considered to be as late as the second century B.C. It is noteworthy that in the entire book there is hardly a reference to David which can be clearly assigned to the prophet.

Ezekiel (592–570).

In this prophet we have allusions to David which appear to be Ezekiel's own utterances. They are the following:—

xxxiv. 23, 24. "And I will set up one shepherd over them, and he shall feed them, even my servant David; he shall feed them, and he shall be their shepherd. And I the Lord will be their God, and my servant David prince among them; I the Lord have spoken it."

xxxvii. 24, 25. "And my servant David shall

be king over them; and they all shall have one shepherd: they shall also walk in my judgements, and observe my statutes and do them. And they shall dwell in the land that I have given unto Jacob my servant, wherein your fathers dwelt; and they shall dwell therein, they, and their children, and their children's children, for ever: and David my servant shall be their prince for ever."

In all the above verses David is spoken of as the "servant" of Yahweh. In chapter xxxvii., which refers to a future restoration of the Kingdom, the rule of David is regarded as favourable to the observance of divine law. The "David" here mentioned is not, of course, the actual David, but a new hero of whom the first David is the type. The original David is therefore clearly set forth as an ideal ruler, a pattern for later kings to follow. He is the representative of Yahweh, and governs in accordance with his law.

It is to be noticed that this description of David is the earliest reliable allusion to the king which appears in the prophets. It is written four centuries after his death, and shortly after the kingdom of Judah had been destroyed by the Babylonian power. Ezekiel penned his prophecy on the banks of the Kebar near Babylon.

Zechariah (520 and following years B.C.).

This prophet lived in Canaan about the end of the Exile-century and in the early part of the next. Thus he tells us (i. 1) that the word of the Lord came to him in the second year of Darius, who reigned from 521 to 485 B.C. What he writes is therefore to be dated about 500 years after David's age. The reference to "Satan" (iii. 1) is in accordance with this late date.

The following are the allusions to David :—

xii. 7, 8. "The Lord also shall save the tents of Judah first, that the glory of the house of David and the glory of the inhabitants of Jerusalem be not magnified above Judah. In that day shall the Lord defend the inhabitants of Jerusalem; and he that is feeble among them at that day shall be as David; and the house of David shall be as God, as the angel of the Lord before them."

xii. 10. "And I will pour upon the house of David, and upon the inhabitants of Jerusalem, the spirit of grace and of supplication; and they shall look upon me whom they have pierced : and they shall mourn for him, as one mourneth for his only son, and shall be in bitterness for him, as one that is in bitterness for his first-born."

xii. 12. "And the land shall mourn, every family apart; the family of the house of David apart, and their wives apart."

xiii. 1. "In that day there shall be a fountain opened to the house of David and to the inhabitants of Jerusalem for sin and for uncleanness."

There is nothing in these passages ethically favourable to David. On the one hand, his "glory" is mentioned; on the other, his "house," presumably his descendants, are by inference sinful and unclean, for they are in need of a fountain to be opened to them.

The Books of Kings.

Before investigating the testimony to David's character furnished by these documents, we must attempt to ascertain their date. The narrative is carried up to 560 B.C., the thirty-seventh year of the captivity of Jehoiachin in Babylon, when he was released from prison (2 Kings xxv. 27); but the main redaction is probably not so late as the Exile (597 B.C.). It can hardly, however, be earlier than the reforms of Josiah (622–621 B.C.), for it was not till then that the worship of Yahweh was centralised in Jerusalem, and the provincial high places were abolished. Before Josiah's time, the most religious kings worshipped at the high places without suspicion of evil. But the historian condemns even these. Whatever their virtues and merits, it is said of their reigns : "Howbeit the high places were not taken away." Even the pious Asa, whose "heart was perfect with Yahweh all his days," comes under the censure.

There is, indeed, a passage (2 Kings xviii. 4–6) which assigns to Hezekiah the removal of the high places. The same idea is also put into the mouth of Rabshakeh (ver. 22). But these passages must be regarded with suspicion. The "Book of the Law," "found" by Hilkiah in Josiah's reign, contains the first condemnation of the high places on divine authority. Exodus (xx. 24) distinctly legitimates them.

Elijah rebuilds the fallen altars on the sacred mount of Carmel. Amos and Hosea do not censure the high places. " There is no sound evidence," writes Professor Cheyne, " that Isaiah attacked them "; and the same authority concludes that their destruction by Hezekiah is a detail incorrectly transferred from the reign of Josiah. If this view is accepted, the condemnation of the high places, and the eulogies of David which go with them, are some four centuries later than David's time. Even if we concede the earlier date of Hezekiah's reign, there will still be an interval of 300 years, during which the character of David may have undergone considerable idealization.

The following are the principal allusions to David found in the Books of Kings, excluding, of course, 1 Kings i., ii., which belong to the reign of David, and are mainly written by the Yahwist.

In the early part of 1 Kings, where the reign of Solomon is described, there are many references to David, especially in connection with the building of the temple.

xi. 4. " His heart was not perfect with the Lord his God, as was the heart of David his father." The perfection here mentioned has reference to religion, not to morals. This is clear from the context, in which David is contrasted with Solomon, whose heart is turned to strange gods by his 700 wives. No objection is made to the 700 wives (and 300 concubines) on ethical grounds ; the censure is directed against the idolatry into which they seduced him. "For it came to pass, when Solomon was old, that his wives turned away his heart after other gods." And again: "And Solomon did that which was evil in the sight of the Lord, and went not fully after the Lord, as did David his father. Then did Solomon build an high place for Chemosh, the abomination of Moab, in the mount that is before Jerusalem, and for Molech, the abomination of the children of Ammon. And so did he for all his strange wives, who burnt incense and sacrificed unto their gods " (vv. 6–8).

The high estimate formed of David appears also in vv. 12, 13, in which Yahweh, after threatening punishment for Solomon's sin, promises to leave one tribe under the rule of Solomon's son, "for David my servant's sake."

xiv. 8. "Thou hast not been as my servant David, who kept my commandments, and who followed me with all his heart, to do that only which was right in mine eyes." Jeroboam is here censured for the use of images, and is contrasted with David, whose merit, as before, consists in his adherence to the cult of Yahweh.

xv. 5. "David did that which was right in the eyes of the Lord, and turned not aside from anything that he commanded him all the days of his life, save only in the matter of Uriah the Hittite." David is here contrasted with Abijam, who indulges in idolatrous practices, or at least does not prevent them. The eulogy reaches a high point. All David's acts are commended, with the one exception. His deceitfulness, his cruelty, his moral cowardice, are tacitly approved. These qualities are not thought to be evil, or, if they are so, they are condoned for the sake of David's religious zeal.

2 Kings xx. 6. "And I will defend this city for mine own sake, and for my servant David's sake." This is in the spirit of 1 Kings xi. 13.

xxii. 2. "And he (Josiah) did that which was right in the eyes of the Lord, and walked in all the way of David his father."

In this part of the narrative we are approaching the time when it is highly probable that all these references to David were written. They appear to come from the same hand; at least, they are similar in expression and in thought. They indicate no growth in the Davidic ideal during the four centuries covered by the history. The earlier descriptions of the hero-king are as glowing and eulogistic as the latest. The writer has formed his ideal, and he applies it as a religious standard to all the kings of the Hebrew monarchies. We catch no glimpse of the stages by which the David of the tenth century developed into the David of the sixth; and the prophets of the period, as we have seen, do not help us to fill the gap. Already by the time of the Captivity, or a little before, David is the model king, the pious servant of Yahweh. But, be it remarked, *the Davidic ideal is still unmoral.* He is zealous for the cult of Yahweh; but throughout the entire history of the Hebrew kings, from Solomon downwards, no hint is given that this ideal monarch, this God-inspired saint, possessed any of the ordinary human virtues. He was not wholly without them, as we have already seen; but the Deuteronomic editor appears to have thought them not worthy of mention.

The Psalms.

We have already concluded that none of the Psalms can be safely assigned to David. The evidence that led us to this result is strengthened by our study of David as he is mirrored in the most ancient parts of the Books of Samuel and Kings. The historical David of the Judaic document and the traditional David of the Psalms are frequently in violent contrast with each other. Take the following example in illustration. The fifty-first Psalm has been commonly believed to be the expression of David's penitence after his sin with Bathsheba. The ideas, however, are those of an age far in advance of David's. The deep conviction of sin impregnating this Psalm does not appear in any of the more ancient documents. The theology, too, is of a type which we do not find earlier than the time of Isaiah. Take verses 16 and 17: "For thou delightest not in sacrifice, else would I give it: thou hast no pleasure in burnt offering. The sacrifices of God are a broken spirit; a broken and a contrite heart, O God, thou wilt not despise." Compare this with 1 Sam. xxvi. 19: "If it be the Lord that hath stirred thee up against me, let him accept (*Heb.*, smell) an offering." It is inconceivable that the barbarian chief who held the primitive belief

that the deity could be placated by the smell of ✓
burning flesh should have uttered the lofty and
spiritual conceptions of the Psalm.   This incon-
gruity seems, indeed, to have struck the mind of
a post-Exilic editor, who awkwardly attempts to
combine the two Davids, and contradicts verse 16
by adding verses 18 and 19.   Thus : " Thou hast
no pleasure in burnt offering," is followed by
" Then shalt thou delight in the sacrifice of
righteousness, in burnt offering and whole burnt
offering: then shall they offer bullocks upon
thine altar."

The late dates of the Psalms are now admitted
by all critics.   That any of them are pre-Exilic
is scarcely probable, while some of them are a
late as the second century B.C.   The following
are the allusions to David which bear upon our
inquiry :—

lxxviii. 70–72. This Psalm is written with a
strong Judaic bias.   Ephraim is repeatedly condemned ; but Judah is the chosen tribe, and
Mount Zion the one holy place.   The climax of
the whole is the choice of David as Yahweh's
" servant."   He is brought from the sheep-fold
" to feed Jacob his people, and Israel his inheritance.   So he fed them according to the integrity
of his heart."   This description is of little definite value.

lxxxix. 19 to end.   Here we have a long
account of Yahweh's favour to David ; but it
does not throw much light on the moral character
of the king.   The blessings promised to him
and his seed, and the penalties denounced,

have reference to Yahweh's "judgements" or "statutes" or "commandments"; but we are not told whether these laws are ethical or merely ceremonial.

cxxxii. This Psalm is similar in style and spirit to the last.

We have next to consider what information is afforded by the titles of the Psalms. The men who inserted these titles, if they believed they were doing so accurately, must have considered that David's mental and moral nature was consistent with the thoughts and emotions expressed in his writings. Their belief in the Davidic authorship is thus, in a general way, an indication of the estimation in which David was held in the age in which the titles were prefixed. We must, therefore, glance at the Davidic Psalms, selecting passages of a specifically ethical significance.

v. 6. This verse condemns lying, bloodthirstiness, and deceit.

xv. Here we have a picture of one fit to dwell in God's "holy hill." He is upright, works righteousness, speaks truth in his heart, slanders not, does no ill to his friend, despises reprobates, swears to his own hurt, puts not out money to usury, does not take reward against the innocent.

xix. 12. This passage expresses the desire to be cleansed from secret faults.

xxiv. 4 commends the possession of clean hands and a pure heart.

xxxiv. 13 exhorts to keep the tongue from evil and the lips from speaking guile.

xxxvii. 21 considers it righteous to deal graciously and give.

xli. 1 declares the reward of him who considers the poor.

li. 6 and 10 pray for truth in the inward parts, for a clean heart, and a right spirit.

ci. condemns base things, a froward heart, private slandering of a neighbour, a proud heart, and the worker of deceit.

These extracts are sufficient to prove that at a late period of Hebrew history, probably in post-Exilic times, the editors of the Psalms who prefixed the titles believed that David uttered the preceding sentiments. They, therefore, regarded him as a man of eminent ethical qualities. Comparing their estimate with that which we have extracted from the oldest authorities, we perceive that the original David has acquired many new virtues. He has become an exceptionally righteous man. His ideal is not, perhaps, so high as ours; but it is probably the highest that had been formed in the period covered by the Old Testament writings.

The Books of Chronicles.

It is generally conceded that these are among the latest writings of the Old Testament. According to Professor Robertson Smith and Canon Driver, two leading members of the conservative school of critics, they are to be dated at least two generations after Ezra, and are probably later than 300 B.C. The writer of the books surveys the history of Israel from the standpoint of the post-Exilic age. He has "a Levitical habit of mind." Israel is to him a Church rather than a nation. The religious and sacerdotal elements pervade his writings. He makes history adapt itself to an idealizing motive. Thus, in 1 Kings xv. 14 and xxii. 43, Asa and Jehoshaphat did not abolish the high places; but the Chronicler (2 Chron. xiv. 5 and xvii. 6) declares that they did. In the same spirit, he assigns to David the Levitical organization of his own (post-Exilic) time, whereas the Books of Samuel and Kings know nothing about the Levites. In 2 Sam. vi. David brings up the ark of Yahweh to Jerusalem, offers sacrifices, and blesses the people, without the aid of priest or Levite. The author of the Chronicles, however, associates with the transfer of the ark (1 Chron. xiii., xv., xvi. 1–6) an elaborate sacerdotal organization, in which the Levites take a leading part. Indeed, he goes so far as to put into the mouth of David the assertion that the death of Uzza was due to the neglect of an ordinance that the Levites only should bear the ark (1 Chron. xv. 13). We cannot hesitate to accept the narrative in Samuel as more trustworthy than the statements of an author writing some *seven centuries* after the events which he sets himself to describe. The Books of Chronicles are not, therefore, to be received as genuine history.

The David of the Chronicles is a very different person from the David of the Judaic document. Robertson Smith does not hesitate to describe the former as a "liturgical dilettante." This will be considered no exaggeration by those who will carefully read the twenty chapters (1 Chron. x.-xxix.) devoted to David by the Chronicler. More than half of these are mere ritualism. The King of Israel is represented to be as fastidious about church furniture, church music, holy orders, and sacraments as a modern High-Church curate. So strong is the sacerdotalism of the writer that he alters the original statement that " David's sons were priests" (2 Sam. viii. 18) to "the sons of David were chief about the King" (1 Chron. xviii. 17). It is offensive to his priestly spirit that any, even the King's sons, save the sacred tribe of Levi, should be permitted to minister in holy things.

The priestly ideal of the Chronicler is certainly not one to command the admiration of modern moralists. It is, however, accompanied by a clear advance in ethics, whether indigenous or derived. Hence we find a distinct improvement in the character assigned to David in the Chronicles. His earlier life, stained by many acts of dubious morality, is omitted. Not a word is said about the sin with Bathsheba or the murder of Uriah. The history of David's court (2 Sam. xiii.-xx.), one of the most natural and probable sections of Hebrew lore, is left out, possibly because it exposes too severely the weaknesses of the royal father, and does nothing to favour sacerdotalism. For the first time in the Hebrew historical books there emerges a revulsion from blood-guiltiness. David wished to build a house for Yahweh, but was refused. In Samuel no reason is assigned for the prohibition; but the Chronicler gives the reason. It is because David was a man of blood. In his exhortation to Solomon to build a house for the national deity, David is reported as saying (1 Chron. xxii. 8) : "But the word of the Lord came to me, saying, Thou hast shed blood abundantly, and thou hast made great wars : thou shalt not build an house unto my name, because thou hast shed much blood upon the earth in my sight." The subsequent history of Judah, as narrated in the Books of Maccabees and Josephus, does not reveal any great respect for human life ; but it was at least a step in advance that excessive blood-shedding had come to be regarded as evil.

A higher ethical ideal appears also in the prayer for Solomon attributed to David (1 Chron. xxix. 10–19). He recognises that Yahweh tries the heart, and has pleasure in uprightness. He desires that Solomon may have a perfect heart to obey the commandments, the testimonies, and the statutes of Yahweh. These sentiments are in the spirit and letter of the Deuteronomist and of the "Davidic" psalms.

The First Book of Maccabees.

This document, which stands far above the other books of the Maccabees in historical value, was probably written between 140 and 125 B.C. It, therefore, comes later than the Chronicles by

100 to 150 years. The only reference to David in this book is of some interest. It runs thus: " David, for being merciful, possessed the throne of an everlasting kingdom " (1 Macc. ii. 57). The pious Jew who penned these words presumably had access to the same Old Testament as ours. He must have read of the massacre of the Geshurites and the execution of the descendants of Saul, yet he selects mercifulness as the most eminent of David's virtues. Was the writer's bias in favour of the great Hébrew hero so strong that he was determined to see no dark shades in his picture ? Or was it that, even as late as the Maccabean age, mercy was so rare a quality that even a faint gleam of it shone with overpowering lustre ? Probably both causes were operative. That the Jews of the post-Exilic age idealized their greatest king we have already seen ; and that mercy was little known in the period of the Maccabees is clearly proved by the very history from which our extract is taken.

The New Testament.

In the Gospels David appears fully idealized. The Messiah, who was expected to restore the departed glories of the Jewish kingdom, was to be of the seed of David. This belief was current long before the time of Christ ; and when the Prophet of Nazareth had impressed his personality upon many of the Jewish people, he was recognised by his disciples as the Messiah, and was hailed by the multitude as the " Son of David." So lofty was the popular ideal of David that to be acknowledged as his lineal descendant was regarded by two of the evangelists as among the leading claims of Jesus to the Messiahship. Matthew and Luke place in the forefront of their Gospels the genealogies which were supposed to prove that Jesus was the son of David. Not even the later stories that denied to Joseph the real fatherhood of Jesus could displace these genealogies, contradictory as they were to the dogma of the Virgin Birth.

Jesus himself appeals to the example of David in justification of his relaxation of the Sabbath law. " Have ye not read what David did when he was an hungred, and they that were with him; how he entered into the house of God, and did eat the shewbread, which it was not lawful for him to eat, neither for them that were with him, but only for the priests ? " (Matt. xii. 8, 4; Mark ii. 25, 26; Luke vi. 8, 4). The Prophet of Nazareth thus recognises David as a spiritual authority so august as to entitle him to appear as the model of the Messiah himself. Idealism could hardly be carried higher, unless David had been raised to deity—a process which was, of course, impossible among a people so rigidly monotheistic as the Jews, common enough as it was in the mythology of Aryan peoples.

The Acts of the Apostles contains numerous references to David as a divinely-inspired authority. We may notice the following :—

i. 16. "Brethren, it was needful that the Scripture should be fulfilled, which the Holy

Ghost spake before by the mouth of David concerning Judas."

ii. 25. "For David saith concerning him, I beheld the Lord always before my face," etc.

ii. 29, 30. "The patriarch David......being therefore a prophet," etc.

xiii. 22. "And when he had removed him, he raised up David to be their king ; to whom, also, he bare witness, and said : I have found David, the son of Jesse, a man after my heart, who shall do all my will."

xv. 16. "After these things I will return, and I will build again the tabernacle of David, which is fallen." These words, quoted from Amos, are applied by the apostle James to the establishment of Christianity, which is thus regarded as a revival in a spiritual sense of the kingdom of David.

In the Epistle to the Romans, the writer tells us that Jesus was born of the seed of David (i. 3), and he elsewhere quotes the "Davidic " Psalms as of divine authority.

The Epistle to the Hebrews contains many allusions to David. The utterances of David in the Psalms are regarded as equivalent to the declarations of the Holy Ghost. Thus, the passage, " To-day, if ye shall hear his voice, harden not your hearts," is assigned to David in one place (iv. 7), and to the Holy Ghost in another (iii. 7). David is also mentioned among the list of worthies in the eleventh chapter.

In the Book of the Revelation, Jesus is said to hold " the key of David " (iii. 7) ; he is called

" the root of David " (v. 5), and " the root and offspring of David " (xxii. 16).

We have thus glanced rapidly at the stages of the process by which a successful chieftain, the ruler of a petty Semitic State, is transformed into one of the great saints of history. Had David been a Greek or a Hindoo, he would, probably, have found a place in a national pantheon, side by side with Heracles or Krishna. First, he becomes a model king, a faithful and zealous worshipper of the national deity. Then he appears as a writer of sacred poems, in which he breathes the spirit of a devout pietist. Later on, or perhaps partly contemporaneously, he figures as the creator of a complex sacerdotal system, the holy patron of a national Church, whose organization he takes a large share in elaborating. By this time the defects and vices of the real David have been sloughed away. He is even represented as a model of mercifulness. Later on he emerges as the chief saint of Jewish history. The Prophet of Nazareth derives from him his claim to Messiahship, and appeals to his authority as an interpreter of divine law. His words are repeatedly quoted by the apostles of the Christian Church as the very voice of the Holy Ghost. In the last echo of revelation he who is " the bright, the morning star," also calls himself " the root and offspring of David." Even the great figure of Moses hardly stands higher in the New Testament record than the royal David. Such a historical idealization is one of the most curious problems in the evolution of

Semitic religion, and demands our most careful attention. Some explanation of the problem will now be attempted.

Division 2.—THE CAUSES OF THE IDEALIZATION.

Preparatory: Examples from History.

Before entering upon the causes of the idealization, it will be of interest to study the process of beatification in later ages. I select the following well-known names :—St. Constantine the Great, St. Edward the Confessor, St. Thomas of Canterbury, and King Charles the Martyr. These men stand in, or near, the grade of sainthood. What were they originally, and what were their claims to beatification ?

Constantine the Great did not attain to the rank of an œcumenical saint; but the Russians, and at one time the Latins themselves, sought to raise him to that honour; while the Greeks, according to Gibbon, actually celebrate his festival as a saint, and seldom mention his name without adding the title, "Equal to the Apostles."[1] But, what was his real character? Gibbon asserts[2] that in his old age he degenerated into "a cruel and dissolute monarch." And again: "As he gradually advanced in the knowledge of (Christian) truth, he proportionally declined in the practice of virtue; and the same year of his reign in which he convened the

[1] *Decline and Fall* (1838), ii. 465 and note. [2] *Ibid.*, ii. 327.

Council of Nice was followed by the execution, or rather murder, of his eldest son."[1]   Even the orthodox Mosheim concedes:[2] " It must be confessed that the life and actions of this prince were not such as the Christian religion demands from those who profess to believe its sublime doctrines."   Again, when defending the emperor against the charge of insincerity, he refers to " the crimes of Constantine."[3]   The writer of the article, " Constantine," in the *Encyclopædia Britannica*, remarks that his later years were " disgraced by a series of bloody deeds that have left an indelible stain on the emperor's memory." Further proof of Constantine's immoral life, especially in his later years, is unnecessary. How came it that this wicked man has been idealized into a saint by the Eastern Church, and advanced to almost equal rank by the Western ?   The answer is plain and simple. He was the first Christian emperor. He took the Church of Jesus under his protection, he raised it to be the religion of the empire, he admitted its priests to his friendship, and conferred upon many of its members high offices of State. The ministers of the Church would have been more than human had they not yielded to these seductions. They returned the emperor's support and favour by winking at his vices, by flattering his weaknesses; by lauding as a divine piety his politic patronage of the new religion. The Eastern Christians went further in adulation

---

[1] *Decline and Fall*, ii. 464.   [2] *Eccl. Hist.*, i. 322.
[3] *Ibid.*, i. 323.

than their Western brethren; for the Greek
mind was prone to exaggeration, and the emperor's selection of an Eastern site for his new
metropolis flattered the Greeks as much as it
mortified the Romans. It is no wonder that the
founder of Constantinople was beatified by the
Eastern Church.

We pass to Edward the Confessor, an acknowledged saint of the Catholic Church. "All his
virtues," says Freeman,[1] " were those of a monk,
all the real man came out in his zeal for collect-
ing relics, in his visions, in his long religious
exercises, in his gifts to churches and monas-
teries, in his desire to mark his reign, as its
chief result, by the foundation of his great Abbey
of St. Peter at Westminster." The pursuit of
these hobbies alternated with pleasures of a less
harmless kind. The Confessor delighted in the
excitements of the chase, followed in the ancient
cruel fashion. "Once, we are told, a churl
resisting, it well may be, some trespass of the
king and his foreign courtiers over an Englishman's freehold, put some hindrance in the way
of the royal sport. An unsaintly oath and an
unkingly threat at once rose to the lips of Edward:
'By God and his Mother, I will hurt you some
day, if I can.'"[2] The above sketches set before
us a self-indulgent creature, scarcely worthy,
judged by modern standards, to figure as a
country clergyman. Had he not lived in a
dark and superstitious age, and devoted royal

---

[1] *Norman Conquest*, ii. 24.   [2] *Ibid.*, 26.

wealth and power to the interests of the clergy, he would have won no sainthood.

Thomas of Canterbury is another example of how canonization was purchased by service to the Church. Before his appointment to the primacy, Becket was notoriously an immoral man. His elevation merely altered the direction of his self-seeking energies. As Archbishop, his efforts were devoted to exalting his own power, and asserting for the clergy invidious and dangerous privileges. He provoked the indignant barons to murder, which the Church glorified as martyrdom. Miracles were conveniently wrought at his tomb, and sealed his claim to beatification.

The semi-canonization of King Charles the First shows us the saint-making process under more modern conditions. The records of his life are so abundant that we can see exactly why a bad king was idealized. We know that he was treacherous to his friends: witness his betrayal of Strafford. We know, too, that in his public transactions he was wont to break his word without scruple. His double-dealing was the despair of his most devoted followers. Yet the pietist, Keble, could write of him :—

> "And there are aching, solitary hearts,
>   Whose widow'd walk with thought of thee is cheered,
> Our own, our royal Saint: thy memory rests
>   On many a prayer, the more for thee endear'd."

This tribute was doubtless the expression of sincere feeling; yet how wide the contrast with the historical estimate! The poetic Church

priest sees the slain king as he wants to s
him. A mass of ugly facts is hidden by a veil
of domestic virtues, intershot with strands of
pietism, and dyed with the glorious hues of
martyrdom. Thus the shifty Charles Stuart
becomes as much a saint as a Protestant Church
can make him.

In all these examples we have seen that a high
moral character was not essential to sainthood.
Beatification was the reward of services to the
Church. It was a *quid pro quo*.

The hero-worship of modern Englishman and
mediæval Greek is thus seen to throw light upon
the hero-worship of ancient Hebrewdom. The
idealizing of David is less clearly ascertained,
because the documentary evidence is less free
from mythopœic distortion. Had David's life
and career been written by a contemporary
Thucydides or Hallam, our study would have
been comparatively simple, and our results more
certain. As it is, we can only venture to present
suggestions which, it is to be hoped, will help us
to reach a high probability.

First Cause: David's Military Success as a Proof
of Divine Approbation.

David was to Israel what Bruce was to
Scotland, what Frederick the Great was to
Prussia. He united the discordant tribes
under one sceptre. Then he threw off the
yoke of the Philistines, subdued Edom, Moab,
and the country of the Ammonites, and extended
his kingdom, or at least his suzerainty, to an

unknown distance to the north-east. His empire was petty enough compared with the dominions of the kings of Egypt and Assyria; but to the Hebrews, accustomed to the adventures of small clans, the new kingdom was magnificent. David's career of victory raised the national patriotism to a high pitch of enthusiasm. No Hebrew prince before him had ruled over one-third of the territory acquired by his sword. But the glory quickly passed. On David's death, his empire began to fall to pieces, till only the little Judæan kingdom remained, and even that was swept away by the Babylonian avalanche. Then the bands of exiles who hung their harps upon the willows of Babylon looked fondly back upon their vanished past, and dreamed dreams of a second David, who should restore the throne of the first.

But military glory alone could not grow into an ethical ideal. An eighteenth-century Frederick, to be idealized into a New Testament David, must be placed in David's environment. To understand the idealization of David we must keep clearly in mind the great fundamental theological conceptions of the Hebrews:— (1) That the rule of their national deity was confined to the present life; (2) that the punishments and rewards of his code were purely temporal; and (3) that the only criterion of moral conduct was the material penalty, or the material blessing, which followed it. These thoughts pervade Hebrew history. The measure of the goodness of the patriarchs was the amount of temporal prosperity they acquired. When the people were victorious in battle it was because Yahweh approved of them; while defeat was the result of his displeasure. Saul and his dynasty were extinguished on Mount Gilboa as the punishment of his disobedience to the divine command. The kings who followed David in the northern kingdom establish their families on the throne on the condition that they are obedient to Yahweh; the kings of Judah are continued in the Davidic line on account of the merits of their great Founder, " for my servant David's sake."

It was this misconception of moral government that so grossly misled the friends of Job. Because he had suffered misfortune they inferred that he must have been wicked. The same belief prevailed in a later age, when the Jews of the time of Christ attributed special sinfulness to those upon whom the tower of Siloam fell. The superstition, indeed, is not yet dead. It emerged some years ago in a sermon by the Vicar of Shrewsbury, who ascribed the fall of his church-spire to the wickedness of those who had erected in the town a memorial to Charles Darwin; and has more recently re-appeared in the utterances of certain English ecclesiastics, who made our national sins responsible for our early failures in the Boer war.

These materialistic conceptions were in full vigour in the ages following the death of David. He had been wonderfully successful in war; therefore, it was argued, he must have been

exceptionally holy—holy, that is, as the men of
that period conceived holiness. Yahweh, they
believed, would never have conferred such prosperity except upon a man "after his own heart."
Saul was unfortunate, therefore he was wicked;
David was successful, and was therefore good.
The Hebrews of those ancient times could have
come to no other conclusions. That a sinful
person should enjoy permanent prosperity was
almost inconceivable to them; and when it did
happen it filled them with perplexity and
despair. "When I thought how I might know
this," cried the Psalmist, as he meditated upon
the problem, "it was too painful for me."

The standard of goodness improved from
age to age, and the Davidic ideal improved
with it. The David of the Books of Samuel,
disfigured with many faults, scales off his vices
one after another, till he shines forth in spotless
radiance, worthy to be the ancestor and proto-
type of the divine Messiah.

Second Cause : David's Centralisation of the Cult Secured the Favour of the Priesthood.

David took the first step in the centralisation
of Hebrew worship. Up to his time—indeed, up
to the reign of Josiah—the sanctuaries, or high
places, were numerous. Some of them were of
special sanctity, such as Bethel, Shiloh, Gilgal,
and Beersheba. We may take Bethel as a type.
We are told (Gen. xxviii. 18 f.) the origin of this
sanctuary, how that Jacob took the stone he had
used as a pillow during sleep, " set it up for a

pillar, and poured oil upon the top of it." And he called the name of that place Bethel (*marg. The house of God*). These sacred stones (or houses of El) were probably connected, among the ancient Canaanites, with polytheistic worship, each stone being the dwelling of a god; and it is not unlikely that the Hebrews adopted this cult from their neighbours. The rigid monotheism of a later age was read backward into the records of ancient times, so that all the high places were represented as centres of the worship of the true God, according to the text (Exod. xx. 24), "In every place where I record my name I will come unto thee, and I will bless thee."

David very naturally desired that Jerusalem, his new capital, should be a centre of Yahwistic worship. The selection being made, the next step was to bring up the ark of God, that it might confer upon the new high place a special sanctity, such as it had conferred upon Shiloh in the time of Eli and Samuel. The Judaic document (2 Sam. vi.) describes in vivid language the bringing up of the ark with music and shouting, amid the rejoicings of the whole people. David acts as the high priest at the ceremony, as we have already seen (p. 31). It is evident that the introduction of the ark is regarded by both king and people as an event of supreme importance. While the actual presence of the symbols of deity in the capital of the new empire gave dignity to David's throne, the prestige of a royal metropolis could not fail to react upon the cult, and to confer upon the Davidic high place a dominating position among the sanctuaries of Israel. This connection between the cult and the throne was, indeed, clearly perceived in the age succeeding David's, when the northern monarchy was established. "Jeroboam," we are told (1 Kings xii. 26 *f.*), "said in his heart, Now shall the kingdom return to the house of David : if this people go up to offer sacrifices in the house of the Lord at Jerusalem, then shall the heart of this people turn again unto their lord, even unto Rehoboam King of Judah; and they shall kill me, and return to Rehoboam King of Judah." All rivalry between the northern high places and Jerusalem, however, was terminated by the destruction of the kingdom of Israel, and the city of David remained the chief centre of the Yahwistic cult.

A further evolution was needed to make it *the only* centre. This stage was reached in the reign of Josiah. Under the influence of the Deuteronomic reforms, all the provincial high places were abolished, and Jerusalem became the one sanctuary "where men ought to worship."

This centralisation produced far - reaching changes in the cult. It created a sacerdot aristocracy. The priests of the temple formed a higher grade, supposed to be descendants of Zadok, while the priests of the provincial high places were brought up to Jerusalem, and were constituted an inferior rank of

the priesthood, known as Levites. They
performed humble functions, previously dis-
charged by foreigners, and were not permitted
to minister at the altar. The higher priesthood
acquired increased wealth and consequence from
the concentration of all sacerdotal power in their
hands. In the post-Exilic age the absence of a
secular authority also threw upon them the
duties of government. Thus the Jewish State
was transformed into the Jewish Church. In
Maccabean times the high priest was the
supreme ruler in all matters, spiritual and
secular.

Long after David's age a divine sanction was
sought for the centralisation of religion at
Jerusalem. Hence the theophany described in
2 Sam. xxiv. The angel who has destroyed
70,000 of the people is commanded to sheathe
his sword by the threshing-floor of Araunah the
Jebusite. Here David erects an altar and offers
sacrifices. In 1 Chron. (xxii. 1) we are told that
the King specifically announces: "This is the
house of the Lord God, and this is the altar of
burnt-offering for Israel." I have already (p. 53)
discussed this theophany, and given reasons for
declining to accept its historical accuracy.
Divine sanction or not, the city of David became
the chief centre of Jewish religion; and this
centralisation gave to the sacerdotal order an
enormous accession of power and dignity. It
was, therefore, perfectly natural that the priestly
authors of the later Jewish scriptures should
idealize the character of the king who had laid

the foundation of their greatness. They did for David what the Greek Church did for Constantine; what the Latin Church did for Edward the Confessor and Thomas à Becket; what ecclesiastics in all ages have done for monarchs who have favoured and endowed the priestly caste. The Church of England still describes our sovereigns, whatever their moral character, as "most religious and gracious"; and Russian priests by the thousand pray for victory to follow the banners of the Czar, who won Manchuria by deceit and defended it by slaughter.

PART IV.

DAVID'S PLACE IN COMPARATIVE ETHICS

———

DIVISION I.—DAVID'S PLACE IN HEBREW ETHICS.

IT is a work of extreme difficulty to ascertain the moral standards of the ancient Hebrews. The earlier documents have been so frequently manipulated by later redactors that the analysis of the books into their successive elements is often hypothetical. The doctrinal pragmatism or the preconceptions of the Hebrew writers often destroy the historical value of their work. The Books of Chronicles, for example, stand but little above the rank of a romance designed to glorify the priestly order and their alleged Founder. Fortunately, we are not confined to the Hebrew records. The evidence brought to light by recent researches among the ancient monuments of Egypt and Western Asia gives us much help, and its quantity is increasing almost annually. Some of it has a direct bearing upon Hebrew history, while other portions, by throwing light upon the religion and ethics of peoples closely allied to the Israelites in blood and language, indirectly swell the volume of our knowledge.

It will be of advantage, in the first place, to study the early ethics of the cognate Semitic nations; and, in doing this, it will be desirable to include in our purview their religious ideas; for, if the religion of (say) the Babylonians be found to resemble the Hebrew cult, it will render probable a likeness also in morals between the two peoples, where there may be no direct proof on the Hebrew side. If, for example, we find (as we do) that the early Babylonian gods were non-ethical in character, while, at a later date, they acquired moral natures, we are led to expect a corresponding evolution in Hebrew theology and ethics, and thus we obtain confirmation of what is, perhaps, less clearly set forth in the Hebrew scriptures.

(a) Early Semitic Religion Non-Ethical.

The religion of the ancient Babylonians, according to the Rev. Professor Sayce,[1] was Shamanism, or "Organized Animism," a primitive form of thought which is almost world-wide in its distribution. Professor Sayce describes the Babylonians as believing that spirits inhabit all material objects, living and dead. Their aid is invoked, or their anger is deprecated, by magical incantations uttered by a special caste of medicine-men. The main object of the cult

---

[1] *Religion of the Ancient Babylonians* (Hibbert Lectures, 1887), p. 328.

was to obtain the cure of disease. In this religion " the moral element was wholly wanting."

The Biblical tradition relates that the ancestors of the Hebrews came from the Euphrates valley. In this case, they must, before their migration westward, have shared in the current ethical and religious beliefs. At the time of the emigration, the Babylonian religion had developed into polytheism, and the Abramites must also have been polytheists; but the more primitive types of theology would, more or less, subsist side by side with the newer forms. It is, however, difficult to understand how so barbarous a people as the early Hebrews could have been an offshoot from the Babylonian civilisation of the second or third millennium B.C.

My argument will not be materially affected if we reject the tradition of a direct Mesopotamian origin, and accept the hypothesis that the Hebrews were an Arabian people, whose religious conceptions, when they entered Canaan, were not derived from Babylonia. The Old Testament contains the clearest indications that, until long after the time of David, some of the crudest forms of Nature-worship prevailed, or at least existed, among the Hebrews. Tree-worship was practised. We are told that, on Abram's arrival in Canaan, Yahweh appeared to him at the oak of Moreh (Gen. xii. 6, 7), and, on his return from Egypt, he built an altar to Yahweh by the oaks of Mamre (Gen. xiii. 18). Similar references appear from time to time in the traditions of later patriarchs. Even in the age of the prophets tree-worship still survived. Isaiah (i. 29) declares : " For they shall be ashamed of the oaks which ye have desired "; and, much later, the Deutero-Isaiah speaks of those who "inflame yourselves among the oaks [*marg.*, or *"with idols* "] under every green tree " (Isa. lvii. 5). The cult of sacred stones was also in vogue up to the later prophets, as appears from the Deutero-Isaiah (lvii. 6) : " Among the smooth stones of the valley is thy portion ; they, they are thy lot: even to them hast thou poured a drink-offering, thou hast offered an oblation." Familiar examples of stone-worship are the pillar erected at Bethel by Jacob (Gen. xxviii. 18–22), the stones set up by Joshua at Gilgal (Josh. iv. 20), which formed a cromlech or stone-circle, and the great stone which he erected under the oak at Shechem (Josh. xxiv. 26, 27), a combination of tree and stone worship. The Massebahs, or stone pillars, two of which stood before the temple of Solomon, are repeatedly mentioned in the historical books and the prophets. Of the Asherahs, or wooden symbols of a phallic deity, for which the Hebrew women wove hangings (2 Kings xxiii. 7), and of the sacred wells and mountains, it is needless to speak. The evidence is overwhelming that the Nature-worship of the Hebrews did not differ from that of other Semitic peoples, and the inference is probable that, in the former as in the latter, " the moral element was wholly wanting."

(b) Early Semitic Society Ethical.

It does not follow that, because the moral element is absent from the lower religions, it is also wanting in the lower human societies. It would be impossible for the rudest and simplest communities to hold together without some rules for restraining the selfishness of the individual in the interests of the many. Among the least developed of existing races are the aborigines of central and northern Australia. They wear no clothing and build no houses. They live upon such food as they can obtain in the bush. Scarcely any property exists among them. Totemism is their dominant form of belief. They perform elaborate ceremonies to increase the totem, which is generally a form of food, animal or vegetable, or a useful natural production, such as rain. They can hardly be said to possess a trace of a religion, the nearest approach to one being the propitiation of a mythical snake called the Wollunqua. Yet this primitive race possesses a traditional code of ethics. The law of blood-revenge is in force. No man is allowed to interfere with the wife of another except during the performance of certain magical rites. Obedience to elders is obligatory. The able-bodied must provide food for the aged. Messrs. Spencer and Gillen, from whose recent work[1] the above particulars are extracted, state most positively that they could find no trace among the natives of a belief in a " great moral

[1] *The Northern Tribes of Central Australia*, 1904.

preceptor," such ethical precepts as exist being
inculcated by the old men at initiation.   These
savages have no religion ; that is, they have no
sense of accountability to a higher invisible
power or powers ; yet they have a moral law.

Semitic society, so far back as we can follow
it, was ethical.   Robertson Smith remarks[1] that
" murder and incest, or offences of a like kind
against the sacred laws of blood, are in primitive
society the only crimes of which the community,
as such, takes cognisance."   This code is a limited
one, as all codes must be where the complex
relations of civilisation have not arisen ; but it
implies the recognition of moral law.

We may then conclude that in ancient Semitic
society the people were more moral than their
religion ; and it requires no very profound reflection to explain the seeming anomaly.   Men went
to their gods—their trees or their stones—for
some material benefit, or to be delivered from
some material evil, such as disease or the
weapons of an enemy.   This was the whole
object of worship among the early Semites, even
after polytheism had been developed, as plainly
appears from the older documents of the Bible,
as well as from the monumental inscriptions of
Babylonia, Assyria, and Phœnicia.   But how
could men apply the law of murder or of
adultery to their gods ?   The members of the
kin or tribe were individually responsible to
the community whose interests were bound up

[1] *Religion of the Semites* (1889), p. 399.

with their own; but to whom was the god to be responsible? The spirit inhabiting a stone, or the ancestor haunting a grave, could be responsible to none. A god, like a king in later ages, could do no wrong. He was above all law, and could be judged by no standard. He was neither good nor evil: he was merely a sort of automatic machine, from which a penny in the slot in the form of a magic rite might extract something pleasant.

We cannot speak with certainty of the form of religion which in early Semitic society succeeded fetishism as the highest cult. The worship of the totem-animal may have been an intermediate step to polytheism. We seem to have traces of it in the worship of the bull in Babylonia, of the cherub or winged man-bull of Assyria, and of the golden calf (or bull) and brazen serpent among the Israelites. The taboo of swine's flesh may also point to totemism. But any conclusions we may build upon the slender material at our command are lacking in solidity.

(c) Semitic Polytheism and Monolatry.

Professor Sayce holds[1] that the ethical element entered Babylonian religion under Shamanism, the evil being the first to emerge. The spirits who inhabited all material objects were malevolent, and had to be propitiated by

---

[1] *Rel. Ancient Babylonians*, p. 330. If the spirits were ethical, there was nothing ethical in men's relations with them.

sacrifice or coerced by spell. Then cosmogonic speculation entered, and great creative spirits (gods) were imagined. These possessed good and evil qualities, the good being in the ascendant. They were approached by prayer, and flattered by praise and adoration. Finally, a complicated ritual was evolved, elaborated in minute details, and performed by a priestly caste, organized into various ranks.

Nothing so highly wrought as this final stage existed among the Hebrews previous to the Exile. Under the Judges and early Kings, Israel was in the unelaborated polytheistic phase. The worship of anthropomorphic gods partly superseded the earlier Nature-cult. Teraphim or household gods were possessed, and doubtless worshipped, by David; and even as late as Hosea they were regarded as essential to the national religion (Hos. iii. 4). The word *Elohim*, wrongly translated "God," is a plural, and is believed by Sayce to point to an earlier polytheism. Robertson Smith regarded the elohim of a locality as the total of its sacred denizens. We are told (Exod. vi. 3) that the early patriarchs worshipped a god called "El Shaddai."[1] It was not till the time of Moses that the deity was revealed (Exod. vi. 2 *f.*), who, as Jehovah or Yahweh, became the chief, and ultimately the sole, god of the Hebrew people. After the Exile the monotheism of the Jews grew so rigid

---

[1] Delitzsch (F.) thinks that "El Shaddai" is derived from the Assyrian *sadu* (a mountain), and points to stone-worship.

and exclusive that strenuous efforts were made to destroy the traces of the earlier cults; but it was not found practicable to effect such a drastic revision of the ancient records. The priestly redactor (Exod. vi. 2 f.) represents Yahweh as the same god as was known to the patriarchs under another name, El Shaddai; while the lower cults, which were destroyed by Josiah, are regarded as departures from pure Yahweh-worship rather than ancient survivals. At the time of David the earlier cults had apparently become subordinate to the worship of Yahweh, the national god of the Hebrew people. He was their supreme, but not their only, deity. As Wellhausen points out,[1] Israel was "mono-theistic[2] precisely in the sense" in which Moab, Edom, and Ammon were "monotheistic." Moab had its Chemosh, the Ammonites their Milcom, and the Israelites their Yahweh.

(d) Derivative Origin of the Higher Elements of Hebrew Worship.

Religion and ethics are so closely associated in a certain stage of ancient thought that it would be well to glance briefly at the origin of the higher elements of Hebrew religion before we compare Hebrew ethics with that of other Semites.

It seems to be now generally recognised by scholars that the later forms, at least, of Hebrew

---

[1] *Sketch of the Hist. of Israel and Judah*, 3rd ed., p. 23.
[2] "Monolatrous" would be the more accurate word.

religion are derived from Babylonia. I do not here speak of the cosmogonies, but of the actual cult. And, first, of the national deity, Yahweh. The evidence recently obtained from the ancient monuments of Western Asia appears to establish his derivative origin. Professor F. Delitzsch, the eminent Assyriologist of Berlin University, has pointed out[1] the most striking resemblances between the monuments and parts of the Hebrew Bible, and among these the identity of the Israelite Yahweh and a Babylonian deity is the most important. The Babylonian pantheon included a deity named " Yahu," who possessed substantially all the attributes ascribed by the Hebrews to their " Yahweh." The derivation of the name " Yahweh " from a Babylonian source is, indeed, not absolutely new. Pinches[2] recognised the names " Ya " and " Jawa " in Assyro-Babylonian inscriptions, and the following extracts from *Records of the Past* place the identity beyond reasonable doubt.

On an Assyrian monument,[3] Assur-nasir-pal, king of Assyria about 880 B.C., calls himself " worshipper of Anu, exalter of Yav "; and the Rev. J. M. Rodwell, the translator of the inscription, states that " the god Yav may be the Yaveh of the Moabite stone," " Yaveh " being the Jehovah (Yahweh) of Dr. Ginsburg's translation, whose sacred vessels the Moabite king captured from Israel.

A monolith in the British Museum[4] bears an

[1] *Babel and Bible* (1903). [2] *Enc. Bib.*, col. 3322, note 3.
[3] *Records of the Past*, iii. 42. [4] *Ibid*, iii. 80.

invocation to the great gods of the Assyrian
pantheon.   In this list we find " Yav Jahve."

"El" or " Il," another of the divine names of
the Old Testament, is found on the ancient
monuments.   An inscription of Tiglath Pileser[1]
contains a reference to the " temple of Martu, of
Bel, and of Il."   Nebuchadrezzar, on a monument dating about 600 B.C., refers[2] to "the god
El, the beauty of the sphere," and to someone
" whose names El had proclaimed."   He also
worships " Yav."   Darius I.[3] associates " El "
with the gods Anu and Hea, two chiefs of the
Babylonian pantheon.

Some of the Babylonian gods are not only
identical with Hebrew deities in name, but they
were similar in character.   Sayce[4] draws a
parallel between Yahweh and Assur, the god of
the Assyrians.   Each (1) was a " king above all
gods"; (2) was the national god of a race;
(3) stood by himself without female; (4) was a
" jealous god," more terrible than the Baalim,
who were probably gods of vegetation; and (5)
was a " god of battles."

Non-Hebrew Semites appealed to their gods
for aid in battle in the style ascribed in the Bible
to leaders like Moses and Joshua.   Shalmanezer[5]
speaks thus: "By the mighty forces which
Assur, the lord, gave......I fought with them."
So King Mesha,[6] as recorded on the Moabite

---

[1] *Records of the Past*, v. 21.   [2] *Ibid*, v. 118.
[3] *Ibid*, ix. 95.   [4] *Rel. Anc. Babylonians*, 122–129.
[5] Sayce's *Higher Criticism and the Verdict of the Monuments* (1894), 391.   [6] *Ibid*, 366, 367.

stone, uses language of his god Chemosh strikingly similar to passages in the Old Testament. "Chemosh," he says, "was angry with his land......And Chemosh said to me, Go, seize Nebo upon Israel......And Chemosh drove him (the King of Israel) out before me."

The similarity between prayers on Assyrian monuments and some of the Jewish Psalms is very close. The following[1] is in the dialect of Sumar or Shinar, and belongs to an early period of Babylonian history :—

"My Lord is wroth in his heart, may he be appeased again.

" May God cease from his anger.

" O my Lord, my transgression is great ; many are my sins.

" The forbidden thing did I eat.

" To God I refer my distress ; I utter my prayer.

" O my God, seven times seven are my transgressions ; my transgressions are ever before me."

It will be easier to accept the above evidence when we learn that the other chief elements of advanced Hebrew religion were derived from foreign nations. Thus, Professor Sayce tells us[2] that among Phœnicians and Assyrians there were many festivals and fasts like those of the Jews ; that they had peace-offerings and heave-offerings ; that they dedicated their first-born

---

[1] Sayce's *Fresh Light from the Ancient Monuments* (1884), 158 *f.*
[2] *Ibid.*, p. 67.

and made sacrifices for sin; that they carried about the gods in "ships" like the Hebrew ark; that in front of the images of their gods was placed a table with shew-bread; that their religion forbade the flesh of swine and creeping things; and that in the outer court of the temples were large "seas, like Solomon's, for lustrations." Many of these institutions had come down from the Accadian period, and were, therefore, not only older than the Hebrew settlement in Canaan, but than the supposed emigration of Abram and his followers from their Mesopotamian home.

Professor Sayce[1] further informs us that the Babylonian temple was on the plan of Solomon's. At one end of it was a holy of holies with a veil in front. The sacrifices offered were similar to those of the Jews, the animals being oxen, sheep, and gazelles. There were also offerings of meal and wine. In the Accadian era, which preceded the Babylonian, the sacrifice of children by their fathers was practised, according to the text: "The father will give the life of his child for his sin"; which is echoed in Micah (vi. 7): "Shall I give my first-born for my transgression, the fruit of my body for the sin of my soul?" In a more humane age animals were substituted for children, as represented in the narrative of Abraham offering up Isaac, which is probably of later date than Micah.

The Babylonians, like the Hebrews, offered

---

[1] *Rel. Anc. Bab.*, p. 64 *f.*

hymns and prayers; they practised ablutions with water; and their priests wore a peculiar dress. They also recognised the well-known distinction between things clean and unclean.

This evidence could be greatly enlarged, but the above examples are sufficient to show the close resemblance between Babylonian and Hebrew religion. Either the Hebrew religion was evolved independently, or was derived from neighbouring countries, especially Babylonia. Its derivative origin appears to be proved by the following considerations :—

1. The Babylonians were a civilised people, with an organized religious system, many centuries before the Hebrews settled in Canaan.

2. An elaborate system of temple-worship did not appear among the Jews before the Exile. In Babylonia they found it already established. On their return to Judæa it was adopted in Jerusalem, and descriptions of it were incorporated with the older documents of the Hebrew scriptures, or given in the Books of Chronicles, Ezra, and Nehemiah.

3. The Sabbath is acknowledged to have been an Accadian institution, and was, therefore, in force in Babylonia centuries, probably millenniums, before the alleged delivery of the law on Sinai. Yet it is not mentioned in Judges, Joshua, or Samuel. It is named only twice in Kings, and thrice in the pre-Exilic prophets (Amos viii. 5; Isa. i. 13; Hosea ii. 11). On the return from Babylonia, however, the Sabbath has become one of the most important of Jewish

institutions. It is mentioned frequently in the Pentateuch, Chronicles, Nehemiah, Ezekiel, and Deutero–Isaiah. The Jews of the time of the Maccabees permitted themselves to be slain without resistance rather than violate the holy day. Why this change? We may fairly infer that the Jews learned their extraordinary reverence for the Sabbath from their Babylonian neighbours during the Captivity.

4. The Hebrew cosmogonies, the accounts of the Fall and the Deluge, are too similar to inscriptions on Babylonian cylinders to have been independently originated.

The derivation of the higher elements of Hebrew religion from the Babylonians suggests an *à priori* probability of a derivative origin for the more advanced Hebrew ethics.

(e) Ethics of the Non-Hebrew Semites in the Polytheistic Stage.

(1) ETHICS OF THE CULTS.

One of our highest authorities on Semitic religion, and a conservative theologian, asserts :[1] " It is quite certain that it (holiness) in ancient Semitic religion has nothing to do with morality and purity of life," and he instances[2] the *kedeshoth* or harlots connected with temple-worship, to whom the words " sacred " and " holy " were applied. This " ancient " religion

[1] W. Robertson Smith, *Religion of the Semites*, p. 132.
[2] *Ibid.*, p. 133.

was far advanced beyond the primitive stage, for "sacred" prostitution was certainly in existence as late as the prophet Hosea (iv. 13): "They sacrifice upon the tops of the mountains, and burn incense upon the hills, under oaks and poplars and terebinths, because the shadow thereof is good: therefore your daughters commit whoredom and your brides commit adultery." Compare Deut. xxiii. 18 : "Thou shalt not bring the wages of a whore......into the house of the Lord thy God for any vow"—where the prohibition implies the practice.

Robertson Smith's conclusion is quite justified by the ancient monuments. The worship offered to Assyrian and Babylonian deities was usually quite unethical. As a type we may take an inscription of Tiglath-Pileser.[1] He sacrifices young animals to "my Lord Assur." He prays that Anu and Vul may preserve him in power, preserve the men of his government, bring rain, and make him victorious.

Nebuchadrezzar[2] builds a house for the god Yav, "who confers the fertilising rain upon my land."

Sargon[3] (720 B.C.) calls himself a "pious king"; yet by his own description he appears to have been an extremely wicked man and a great robber. People who support him are said to "follow the road of righteousness." He immolates victims to obtain pardon of the gods,

---

[1] *Records of the Past*, v. 21.   [2] *Ibid.*, p. 123.
[3] *Ibid.*, vii. 25 *f.*

and asks for "a happy existence, a long life, an illustrious descendance, and the constancy in victory."

The unethical character of the deities is seen still more clearly in an earlier, but by no means a primitive, stage of thought. An Accadian liturgy,[1] considered by Sayce, the translator, to be older than 2000 B.C., and to contain most of the primary articles of the Accadian faith, is absolutely unethical, and almost entirely non-religious. It is supposed to be spoken by the god Ea, one of the three members of the Accadian trinity. It is a boastful panegyric on himself: "I am Lord......My mighty weapon, which like an orb smites in a circle the corpses of the fighters, I bear.......The striker of mountains, my murderous weapon of Anu, I bear......," and so on to several pages.

The following[2] Accadian psalm, anterior to the seventeenth century B.C., when the Accadian language became extinct, has a more religious complexion. It is the expression of a penitential soul. The sins confessed are—(1) Profaning the name of the deity; (2) eating forbidden food; and (3) trampling upon that which is forbidden. These offences were committed unknowingly, yet the sinner bewails his guilt in the most distressful terms. He cries:—

"O my Lord, my transgression is great, many are my sins......

"I lay on the ground, and no man seized me

---

[1] *Records of the Past*, iii. 127.   [2] *Ibid.*, vii. 151.

by the hand; I wept, and my palms none took......

"I cried aloud, and there was none that would hear me; I am in darkness and trouble......

"My transgressions are before me; may thy judgment give me life."

This psalm is very suggestive. The soul of the penitent is overwhelmed with grief; yet what has he done? He has merely offended against the *amour propre* of his gods. May not some of our penitential Psalms involve a like interpretation? The thought, the very expressions of this psalm, are closely paralleled in the Hebrew Psalter.

Professor Sayce gives us[1] a translation of a Babylonian Saints' Calendar. It is written in Assyrian, but "borrowed by the Semites from the old Turanian (Accadian) theology and science," and, therefore, expressing the religious conceptions of a date at least as old as 1700 B.C. It shows that each day in the year had its special deity or patron-saint. Among other points of interest is its revelation of the origin of the Hebrew Sabbath. The seventh was an unlucky day, on which the king fasted, did not change his clothes, take medicine, or transact any business. Other injunctions laid down in the Calendar are "closely analogous to the Sabbatical injunctions of the Levitical law and the practice of the Rabbinical Jews." But, so far as we can judge

[1] *Records of the Past*, vii. 157.

by the Calendar, the Accadian religion was purely unethical. It was made up of worship, ritual, sacrifices, and abstinences. The Calendar says not a word of the service of man—not a single word !

(2) ETHICS OF THE MAGICIANS.

To the Accadian epoch belong some hymns of a distinctly ethical tone. They are addressed to Samas, the Sun-god. The following extracts[1] are of great interest :—

"Lord, illuminator of the darkness, who piercest the face of darkness, merciful god, who settest up those that are bowed down, who sustainest the weak......He who establishes truth in the thoughts of the nations is thyself. Thou knowest the truth, thou knowest what is false. Sun, justice has raised its head ; Sun, falsehood, like envy, has spoken calumny......Sun, the supreme judge of heaven and earth is thyself...... Sun, the supreme judge of the countries is thyself. The Lord of living beings, the one merciful to the countries is thyself......Thou who annihilatest falsehood, who dissipatest the evil influence of wonders, omens, sorceries, dreams, evil apparitions."

The strong contrast between the lofty ethics of these hymns and the cut-and-dried ritualism of the Saints' Calendar, both of which, it must be remembered, are older than 1700 B.C., is accompanied by a difference of origin. The Calendar is almost certainly a priestly composi-

---

[1] *Records of the Past*, xi. 123, 124.

tion, designed for the use of temple-officials and other persons of sacerdotal tastes. But the hymns are of the nature of magical incantations, and are so described in their headings. In one place the writer calls himself "the magician, thy obedient servant."

The Serpu[1] series of exorcism-tablets contains similar evidence. A person has been bewitched. The sins which may have incurred the malign spell are the following. The sufferer may have (1) sinned against his god; (2) dishonoured his father and mother; (3) used false weights or money; (4) approached his neighbour's wife, shed his blood, or stolen his garment. Side by side with ethical causes the tablets recognise the influence of mere magic. Inquiry is made whether the patient has in any way caught the mischief by communication with a bewitched person. This survival of the lower amidst the higher subtracts nothing from the force of the evidence that in polytheistic Babylonia the magician recognised ethical causation, while in such an important document as the Saints' Calendar the priest ignored it.

Lenormant[2] points out that it is the later magical litanies which contain the idea of the punishment of sin by disease, and the necessity of repentance; but it must be kept in mind that, even at a still more recent epoch, the theology of Assyria and Babylonia was comparatively

---

[1] *Enc. Bib.*, "Magic." col. 2898.
[2] *Chaldæan Magic*, p. 141.

unethical, as shown in my last section. It is a very suggestive fact that magic, which we commonly associate with immoral and degrading practices, should even in this remote age be expressive of a comparatively advanced morality. What is the explanation?

Some light is thrown upon the question by the true definition of magic. According to the high authority of Dr. Frazer,[1] magic proper is a kind of crude science, the effort of primitive men to influence nature directly, religion coming in when they appeal to gods to help them. "Magic," says Adolph Bastian, "is the physics of mankind in a state of nature," thus agreeing with Frazer. The ancient magicians, like the modern Australian savage, applied the logical methods of similarity and contiguity; but they applied them in a childish way. By imitating Nature they thought to influence it. They sprinkled water on a man's body to cleanse his soul. To reduce the virulence of disease they brought a plant into connection with the sick man, and then said: "As this plant withers, so also shall be the spell"; for they believed, as does the modern savage, that it is evil magic which causes sickness. Some of the magical remedies were sacred texts or potent numbers; but others were minerals or vegetable drugs, which might really produce a medicinal effect. Thus magic in course of time passed into true medical science.

---

[1] *Golden Bough*, 2nd ed., i., 61.

This attempt to bring man into touch with nature, defective as it was, could not but give him a clearer perception of truth than his theology, which was concerned with imaginary beings. The most haphazard physical experiment on a sick man's body was more hopeful of result than appeals to Bel or Istar. It is true that magic did not remain absolutely unadulterated with religion. It came to be mixed up with belief in spirits, and afterwards in gods; so that the incantations of the magician were often merely spells for compelling the spiritual powers to intervene; but even these efforts imply belief in a force above the gods, in the existence of laws to which even they must bow.

The primitive belief in magic survived, and it tended to give men a less distorted perception of the universe than they could find in the anthropomorphic inventions of the priest. Thus magic, ridiculous and pernicious as it appears to a more enlightened age, had an ethical tendency, for it contained the germs of truth. In the inscriptions on the ancient monuments it would thus appear that we may discern, however dimly, the beginnings of the great conflict between science and theology.

(3) ETHICS OF THE PEOPLE.

The laws of the Accadians embody clear, if sometimes distorted, views of justice. A tablet,[1]

---

[1] *Records of the Past*, III., 23, 24.

referred by Professor Sayce to " a very remote period," contains the following laws, among others of a non-moral type:—

" His father and his mother (a man) shall not (deny)......

" Everything a married woman encloses she (shall) possess......

" A son says to his mother, ' Thou art not my mother': one shall brand his forehead, deny him the city, and expel him from the house."

Fathers and mothers were to be imprisoned for denying their son. A woman unfaithful to her husband was to be thrown into the river. A man for repudiating his wife was to pay a fine. For killing a slave a fine of a half-measure of corn daily was to be exacted.

A judicial decision inscribed on a Babylonian contract-tablet[1] of the time of the early Accadian Kings contains the following admirable injunctions :—

" Brother to brother should be loving; brother from brother should not turn, should not quarrel; over the whole a brother to a brother should be generous; the whole he should not have."

An ancient Babylonian precept prescribes that, if a king takes bribes to pervert justice, the god Bel brings against him a victorious foe. Another declares that Merodach shall punish an unjust tribute by overthrow and loss of territory. Sayce considers it probable that the document

---

[1] *Records of the Past*, v. 109.

containing these extracts is "based upon an Accadian original, but in its present form it belongs to the Semitic period of Babylonian history." It represents the stage of ethical evolution when theology had become more or less moralised.

The above extracts indicate that long prior to the existence of formulated law in Hebrewdom a comparatively high moral character distinguished the Babylonian people. The facts come out still more clearly in the Code of Hammurabi, discovered in December, 1901. This legislation is of the highest importance for students of ancient ethics, and will be briefly compared with Israelite law in a future section.[1]

(f) Ethics of the Hebrews in the Davidic Age.

(1) ETHICS OF THE CULT.

The conclusion of Robertson Smith, that in early Semitic religion holiness had nothing to do with morality, appears to be applicable to the period covered by the earlier documents of the Old Testament. Dr. Archibald Duff, describing the character of the Hebrew deity Yahweh, bluntly declares[2] that "no particular moral excellence was attributed to him in the period before David." This is a startling statement to issue from a Nonconformist college ; but it is clearly supported by the Hebrew scriptures.

---

[1] It may be more fully studied in Boscawen's *The First of Empires* (1903), Cook's *The Laws of Moses*, etc. (1903), and Chilperic Edwards' *The Hammurabi Code* (1904).

[2] *Theol. and Ethics of the Hebrews* (1902), p. 20.

In the Old Testament the word "holy" is very frequently applied to the deity. He is "glorious in holiness." "Holy, holy, holy, is the Lord of hosts." "Ye shall be holy, for I the Lord your God am holy." Such texts as these abound. But what do they mean? The *Encyclopædia Biblica* tells us[1] "it is certain that Yahweh's holiness and his glory are correlative terms "— that is, his holiness has no ethical quality. So conservative a theologian as Davidson declared that the term "holy" does not express "any particular attribute, but rather the general notion of Godhead." In other words, the deity is "holy," not because he is just or loving, but because he is God. Men become "holy" when they are dedicated to him. Even pots and bells, which certainly do not possess any moral qualities, may be "holiness to the Lord."

The artificial character of holiness in its earlier meanings is frequently seen in the ceremonial parts of the Pentateuch. Take, for example, Lev. xi. 43–45: "Ye shall not make yourselves abominable with any creeping thing that creepeth, neither shall ye make yourselves unclean with them, that ye should be defiled thereby. For I am the Lord your God: sanctify yourselves therefore, and be ye holy, for I am holy: neither shall ye defile yourselves with any manner of creeping thing that moveth upon the earth. For I am the Lord that brought you up out of the land of Egypt, to be your God: ye

---

[1] "Clean," col. 836.

shall therefore be holy, for I am holy." Here
the holiness of the worshipper is purely ceremonial—he must not violate a taboo; and
Yahweh is set forth as his example. The
holiness of the deity is, therefore, as unethical
as the holiness of the man.

Whether or not a god is a moral being must
depend upon his character and behaviour, not
upon the fact that he is divine. We do not admit
that Zeus and Athene are holy when they
prompt men to violate their solemn oaths; and
we can judge in no other way of Yahweh.
What is wrong in a man cannot be right in a
god. Or if the deity does not himself commit
evil, but approves of it, he is equally culpable.
Judging on this principle, what view must we
take of the moral character of Yahweh in the
Davidic age?

We are here met by our old difficulty of
determining which of the narratives truly
describe this period. We have the evidence of
several documents, all of which are later
than David. The Judaic account is nearest to
the events; but we cannot affirm that none of
the later documents contains genuine traditions
of an earlier epoch. In the Pentateuch the
narratives are interwoven in the most perplexing
confusion. This, however, is reasonably certain,
that if the authors of E (the Ephramitic document), D (Deuteronomy), H (the Law of Holiness), and P (the Priestly Code) do not truly
record ancient events, they at least furnish us
with the traditionary accounts of their deity,

K

more or less modified by their own conceptions ; and we may safely infer that they have not *under-estimated* his moral excellence.

If we were to adopt an extreme view of the value of the Pentateuch and the early histories of the Old Testament, and refuse to attribute to them even a substratum of truth, our case would not be materially affected.   We should still have before us a picture of the Hebrew deity as it presented itself to the minds of pious Israelites in the ages succeeding David.   Their god would be their highest conception of moral excellence, so far as they assigned to him ethical qualities at all.   What was this ideal?

THE MORAL CHARACTER OF YAHWEH.

Examples from the Book of Judges.

The Song of Deborah (Judges v.) is commonly regarded as the most important document of the time preceding David.   It is probably the composition of a contemporary of Deborah, if not of Deborah herself.   It presents a vivid picture of life and manners in the time of the Judges, and its archaic cast of thought is in harmony with the age.   The poem is placed in its setting by a Deuteronomistic editor, who has probably added the last verse: " So let all thine enemies perish, O Lord : but let them that love him be as the sun when he goeth forth in his might!" Whatever ethical reflections we can extract from the poem will be of exceptional value.

A careful study of this document suggests that
it reflects an early phase of ethical development.
The following passages will, I think, make this
clear.   Verses 4 and 5 show us Yahweh as a
being of great power, before whom the solid
earth trembles and the clouds drop water.   In
ver. 11 his acts are said to be " righteous," and
the same term is applied to his rule in Israel ;
but we cannot be certain that the word has an
ethical meaning.   The curse against the inhabitants of Meroz (ver. 23) is uttered by " the angel
of the Lord," because they came not "to the
help of the Lord against the mighty."   The
Deity here appears as a warrior contending in
battle, and his curse is the utterance of a dis-
appointed despot, angry with those who failed
to come to his aid, rather than the just wrath of
a moral ruler.   The most significant ethical
indication is given in the glowing eulogy upon
Jael (ver. 24) : " Blessed above women shall Jael
be, the wife of Heber the Kenite ; blessed shall
she be above women in the tent."   Blessed !
Why ?   Because she was a peacemaker ?   Because she was pure in heart ?   No, but because
she had treacherously murdered a man to whom
she had offered hospitality, thus violating even
the defective code of the barbarous Bedween.
The savagery of the poem reaches its most
revolting pitch where the writer gloats over the
anxiety and distress of Sisera's mother.   "Why
is his chariot so long in coming ?" she cries
from the window, as she strains her eyes to
catch the sight of his expected return, knowing

not that he then lay in his blood, slaughtered by
the hand of a woman. " So let all thine enemies
perish, O Lord," adds the pious Deuteronomist,
writing centuries after David's time, so little had
civilisation done to tame the barbarous Hebrew
even in the age of the prophets of righteousness.

But the chief significance of the narrative is
yet to come. Turning to the previous chapter
(iv. 9), we read that " the Lord shall sell Sisera
into the hand of a woman." The treacherous
deed is thus approved, if not instigated, by
Yahweh himself. Furthermore, the writer of
the narrative naïvely admits (iv. 17) that " there
was peace between Jabin the King of Hazor and
the house of Heber the Kenite," so that the
assassination cannot even be palliated as an act
of war. "Sisera lay dead, and the tent-pin was
in his temples. So God subdued on that day
Jabin the King of Canaan before the children of
Israel." Jael's treachery was advantageous to
the Israelites, therefore it is lauded as a glorious
deed, and receives the divine benediction. What
shall we say of the ethics of the people who
embody their ideal in a deity who works his
ends by murder and treachery ?

The career of Abimelech (chap. ix.) throws
some additional light upon the Hebrew conception of the national Deity. The first great
public act of Abimelech was to slay seventy of his
brothers on one stone. This deed is recognised
as wicked by Yahweh, and he is punished by the
millstone thrown by a woman at Thebez. The
men of Shechem, also, suffer penalty for their

complicity in the crime. The sin of Abimelech was an offence against the kin, and was punishable in very early times among the Semites. The ethics of the Deity is, therefore, a mere reflection of the ethics of the clan, and is quite consistent with a low stage of morality. Another idea of great significance emerges in this story. In ver. 23 God is said to "send an evil spirit between Abimelech and the men of Shechem, and the men of Shechem dealt treacherously with Abimelech." The treachery of these men is, therefore, attributed to the instigation of Yahweh himself. We have the same form of thought in the Book of Samuel, the evil spirit which inspired Saul to injure David being sent by God (p. 62). So, also, the lying spirit that enticed Ahab to his ruin comes by command of Yahweh.

The Jephthah incident (xi. 34–40) also indicates an early phase of ethical evolution. Jephthah sacrifices his daughter to his god. The offering is clearly approved by Yahweh, for he gives the warrior success over the Ammonites on his vow to sacrifice as a burnt-offering whatever came from his house to meet him on his return from victory. Within a few centuries of David's death, the idea of a god who delighted in human sacrifice had become too repulsive for the more advanced Israelites. Micah (vi. 7) condemns it, and the Ephraimite document, written in Micah's age, reflects the more humane phase of thought in the account of the abortive sacrifice of Isaac (Gen. xxii.). The divine theophany, in which

Abraham is commanded to substitute a ram, is, in all probability, a mythical explanation of a change which was really due to a softening of human sentiment under the influence of an advancing civilisation.

The Samson episode is in the same vein of thought as the previous examples. This hero is frequently inspired by the spirit of Yahweh, which is always manifested as a spirit of strength. It is because the spirit of the Lord comes mightily upon him that he is able to rend the lion, smite thirty men at Askelon, and snap asunder the ropes by which he was bound. Even his marriage with the Philistine woman, though in later documents marital connections with the heathen are denounced as unlawful, is inspired by Yahweh (xiv. 4), who "sought an occasion against the Philistines." But the most significant ethical indication comes in the great closing scene. Samson prays to be strengthened once more, that he may be avenged upon the Philistines for his two eyes. Throughout his entire career Samson shows himself selfish, sensual, and revengeful; and his last act is one of vengeance. His deity, by answering his prayer and imparting the desired power, gives his sanction to the sanguinary deed.

Examples from the Pentateuch.

The strange scene of the Fall of Man in the Garden of Eden presents us with a view of the character of Yahweh which has been a puzzle and a stumbling-block to thoughtful men in all ages. There is a probation and a fall. Direful penalties are denounced upon Adam and Eve because they have disobeyed a divine command. We cannot judge of the ethical complexion of Adam's sin, since we do not know whether the prohibition was just or unjust. But, however serious the offence may have been, the penalties threatened upon unborn millions are excessive, and, therefore, immoral. A more advanced Hebrew ethic declared that the children should not suffer for the sins of their parents (Deut. xxiv. 16; Ezek. xxxiii.). To make the earth unfruitful, to add to the sufferings of child-bearing, to inflict death upon a sentient world, because one command had been disobeyed by a single pair, are exaggerations of injustice equalling the wildest Oriental dreams. The writer who attributed such conduct to his deity had ethical ideas, it is true; but they were of the coarsest and crudest. All the emphasis is laid upon the disobedience. The thing is wrong because it is forbidden, not forbidden because it is wrong. The essential moral qualities of acts are unrecognised.

The prohibition against eating of the tree of knowledge would, indeed, seem to have been unreasonable. The tree was "good for food"; it was "a delight to the eyes"; it was "to be desired to make one wise." Why should not man desire to become wise? Why should increased knowledge be forbidden? Does this story arise out of the priestly fear of growing enlightenment?

The writer of the narrative seems to have no suspicion that it is the character of Yahweh rather than of Adam that comes under censure. He apparently assumes that a god can do no wrong. This, indeed, is the cardinal defect in the early theology of the Old Testament. The Deity is represented as without moral excellence. He is merely a gigantic Eastern despot, who has no duties to his subjects, and no law but his own will.

The narrative of the Deluge gives us very little ethical information. The great catastrophe is a punishment upon men for their " wickedness," according to J, while P assigns it to their " violence." These terms are too vague to help us. The Babylonian Deluge myth, from which the Biblical accounts are probably derived, is equally indefinite. The city of Surippak is to be overwhelmed with a flood, because it is " evil." Both the Babylonian and the Hebrew narratives leave us in doubt as to the nature of the offences which kindled the anger of the gods. The former, however, is superior in its ethical spirit. Many of the gods are wishful to show mercy to the doomed city, but they are overborne by the warrior Bel. When the vengeance comes,

" Shrieks Istar like a woman in child-birth;
    Cries the great goddess with a loud cry,"

bewailing the doom of her children. The other gods wept with her—

" The gods on their seats sat in tears, covering their lips."

Then, again, when Samas-napisti, the Babylonian

Noah, looks out of the window of the ark and beholds the sea covered with floating corpses—

> "Overcome, I sat myself down, I wept ;
> Over my face flowed my tears."

The Biblical accounts lack these human touches. The writers have no word of pity for the thousands of innocents who could have done nothing to deserve their doom.

But perhaps the most significant light is thrown upon the character of Yahweh by the religious service which followed Noah's exit from the ark (Gen. viii. 20–22). The Deity resolves not to repeat the punishment, being moved to mercifulness not by any ethical considerations, but because he smelt the odour of burning flesh, which was to him a " sweet savour." This conception of pleasing a god by animal sacrifice is imitated from the Babylonian legend :—

> "The gods smelled the odour, the gods smelled the sweet odour.
> The gods swarmed like flies round the master of the sacrifice."

The same gross conception of the divine nature was prevalent in the time of David, who, as we have seen (pp. 62–4), believed that Yahweh might be placated by the smell of a sacrifice, and who himself offered burnt offerings and peace offerings to induce his deity to stay the great plague (2 Sam. xxiv. 25).

The life and character of Moses furnish us with additional knowledge of the nature of his deity. This personage occupies a unique place in Old Testament history. The Deuteronomist

tells us (Deut. xxxiv. 10) that "There hath not
arisen a prophet since in Israel like unto Moses,
whom the Lord knew face to face." He not
only dominates the Hebrew people as their
deliverer and lawgiver, but he has held a place in
the Christian Church second only to the Prophet
of Nazareth. What was the character attributed in the Old Testament to this hero and
saint?

Moses commences his series of interview
with Pharaoh with an untruth. He demands
that the king should let the people go
"three days' journey into the wilderness, and
sacrifice unto the Lord our God" (Exod. v. 3),
intending at the same time to escape entirely
from Pharaoh's power. This deceit is said
(ver. 1) to be commanded by the God of Israel
himself. This example is paralleled by that of
the Hebrew midwives (Exod. i. 18–21). They
give the king a false reason for their inability to
destroy the male children; yet God "dealt
well" with them, and "made them houses."
It is evident that the writers of these two narratives think they are doing no wrong to their
deity by attributing to him the sanction of
deceit.

A lurid light is also cast upon the morals of
Moses by his command to the people to "ask"
of their Egyptian neighbours "jewels of silver
and jewels of gold," with no intention of ever
returning the property. This is done by the
express command of Yahweh, who facilitated the
plundering by giving the people "favour in the

sight of the Egyptians." The writer ingenuously adds : "And they spoiled the Egyptians."

The ethics of the plagues of Egypt reflects the same phase of thought as we saw in the pestilence inflicted upon the Hebrew people because David had ordered a census. A monarch does certain things, and his unfortunate subjects are made to suffer the penalty of his supposed faults. In order that the plagues may be repeated again and again, God is said to harden Pharaoh's heart, and he does so " that ye may know that I am the Lord" (Exod. x. 2). That is to say, direful calamities are inflicted upon tens of thousands of innocent people in order that the Israelites may be satisfied that Yahweh is indeed glorious enough to be their God. These are the credentials of divinity as they were understood by the writers of the earlier Biblical documents ! And Moses, the Man of God *par excellence*, is the means of carrying out a policy which reflects the immoral axiom of the worst despots—that kings are all in all and peoples nothing.

My purpose does not require a minute examination of the character of Moses. I will give one more example. In the Book of Numbers[1] (chap. xxxi.) Moses is commanded "to execute the Lord's vengeance on Midian." The warriors went forth, " and they slew every male," but they " took captive the women of Midian and their little ones." On their return they are met by Moses, who cries : " Have ye saved all

[1] This chapter is by P, and it shows us the low standard of priestly ethics even as late as the Exile.

the women alive?......Now, therefore, kill every
male among the little ones, and kill every woman
that hath known man by lying with him. But
all the women children, that have not known
man by lying with him, keep alive for yourselves." Then a sub-division of the spoil is
commanded, in which Yahweh himself has his
share, a portion of it to be given to Eleazar the
priest and a portion to the Levites. In this
apportionment it is expressly said that Yahweh's
share included a certain number of the persons
—that is, the women. These atrocities and immoralities are attributed by the priestly writer
to Moses, "the Man of God"! Furthermore,
they are repeatedly declared to be perpetrated
by the command of Yahweh.

The examples here given are sufficient to
prove that, in the older Biblical literature, the
Israelites had not advanced beyond gross and
degrading conceptions of their deity. To them
he has not become a good God, scarcely a moral
God at all. Istar, who wept over the doom of
her children, appears more admirable than the
harsh and arbitrary Being who curses the ground
for the disobedience of Adam, and removes the
curse at the sweet savour of a burning sacrifice;
who hardens Pharaoh's heart that he may obtain
a pretext for inflicting worse miseries upon the
unfortunate Egyptian people; and who demands
his share of the plunder of the Midianites, after
having commanded a wholesale massacre of
women and children.

As the god was pictured, so must have been the people who worshipped him as their ideal. *They made him in their own image.*

The Patriarchs.—The characters of the founders of the Israelites are full of ethical interest. Abraham, Isaac, and Jacob appear in the Bible as the model saints of the Hebrew people. To be in Abraham's bosom is to be in Paradise. To sit down with Abraham, Isaac, and Jacob in the kingdom of heaven is to enjoy the fruition of the Christian faith (Matt. viii. 11). They are regarded, not merely as certain of heaven, but as among its most prominent inhabitants. What, then, are the qualifications for so lofty a beatitude? Are they moral or religious? We will first examine the former.

To obtain the right perspective, we must confine ourselves to the Yahwistic narrative. One most interesting result emerges from our inquiries. In the main, *the defects and the virtues of the patriarchs are the defects and the virtues of David.*

One of the least pleasing features of David's character is his *untruthfulness,* and this vice is equally prominent in the three ancients. Abraham, to save his own skin, lies to Pharaoh, declaring that Sarah is his sister. A similar disgraceful story is told concerning Isaac, Abimelech being substituted for Pharaoh. The deceits of Jacob are manifold. He tricks his brother Esau out of his birthright. Later on he lies to his aged father, and cheats Esau out of the paternal blessing. By the cunning trick of the peeled rods, he defrauds his father-in-law, Laban. David's *defective sense of justice* appears in Abraham, when he permits Hagar, bearing his own son in her womb, to be driven into the desert. The failing is still more marked in Jacob, who repeatedly shows himself grossly regardless of the rights of others. *Lack of moral courage* is conspicuous in Abraham and Isaac, when they are willing to surrender their wives to dishonour, if they can secure their own safety. David was *cruel*, and so was Abraham in his behaviour to his concubine Hagar, and in his willingness to sacrifice his son. Hardly less hard-hearted is Jacob's refusal to give food— without a consideration—to his hungry brother. The *sensuality* of David was not wanting in his ancestors. Abraham has two wives and several concubines. Isaac is so greedy for savoury food that he gives his blessing to Jacob in exchange for it. Jacob was content with two wives and two concubines. It is needless to detail the immoralities of Lot, Reuben, and Judah.

The more attractive qualities are also David's. The patriarchs are fond of their near relations. Even Jacob, who lies to his father, wrongs his brother, and tricks his father-in-law, loves his sons, or at least some of them. The fraternal affection of Reuben and Judah to Joseph partially redeems the criminal jealousy of the other brothers. Joseph is the most noble of the patriarchs. His forgiveness of his guilty brothers and his generous behaviour to the whole family remind us of David's magnanimity to Saul in the wilderness of Ziph, and his kindness to Mephibosheth, the son of Jonathan.

Why were these ancient men so highly favoured of heaven? Clearly not because of their moral character. Abraham's great merit is declared to be his obedience to Yahweh. He left his native Mesopotamia, and "obeyed to go out into a place which he was to receive for an inheritance; and he went out, not knowing whither he went" (Heb. xi. 8). He believed the Deity when a son was promised to the aged Sarah. Again he trusted God when, at the divine command, he prepared to offer up Isaac. In these things "Abraham believed God, and it was reckoned unto him for righteousness" (Rom. iv. 3). In modern times such a standard of merit is found only among savages. Dudley Kidd,[1] writing of the South African blacks, informs us that "the highest conception of virtue which most natives can form consists in obedience to the chief." The merits of Jacob also were purely religious. He erects sacred stones to Yahweh, and institutes his worship in a strange land. He is powerful in prayer, and secures blessings for himself in return for his pious ministrations. "If," he stipulates, "God will be with me, and will keep me in the way that I go, and will give me bread to eat, and raiment to put on, so that I come

[1] *The Essential Kafir*, p. 147.

again to my father's house in peace, then shall
the Lord be my God" (Gen. xxviii. 20). And
Jacob's selfish bargain succeeds. Heaven
blesses him. His tricks prosper, his untruths
win benefits, he waxes rich and powerful. But
he keeps his covenant with Yahweh. He
worships him, and obeys his commands. The
moral element in the relations between Jacob
and his God was extremely small. Indeed, it is
difficult to see any virtue at all in obedience to
the commands of an omnipotent deity, without
regard to the moral complexion of the things
commanded.

The Judges.—The assassination of Eglon by
Ehud (Judges iii. 12–30) is peculiarly atrocious.
Ehud secures a private interview with the King
by deceit and hypocrisy. "I have a message
from God for thee," he says, and he thrusts his
sword into the body of his unsuspecting enemy.
Gideon, so highly lauded, was capable of great
savagery. The men of Succoth and Penuel
refuse him food when hungry, and he avenges
himself by cruelly maltreating the elders of
Succoth, and by slaying the men of Penuel.
The moral characters of Abimelech, Jephthah,
and Samson have already been discussed. It
is quite clear that the judges of Israel show no
ethical advance upon the patriarchs.

The First Hebrew Legislation.—While the
examples already cited indicate in a general
way the moral ideas familiar to David and his

contemporaries, we shall find the ethical conceptions of a somewhat later age in the *Book of
the Covenant* (Exod. xxi.–xxiii.), the earliest
extant example of Hebrew legislation. According to tradition, these laws were promulgated by Moses, who is supposed to have lived
about 1300 B.C., and therefore nearly a thousand
years after the Babylonian Code of Hammurabi
(2250 B.C.). Greater probability, however,
attaches to the view that the Book of the
Covenant was not written before the age of the
Yahwist (J) and the Elohist (E), about 850 to
650 B.C., or approximately 1,400 to 1,600 years
after the publication of the Hammurabi Code.
It is not the creation of any person, but, like
the Code, is a summary of customary law, and
it was current in Israel previous to the promul-
gation of the Deuteronomic legislation in the
reign of Josiah (621 B.C.).

The fundamental principles underlying the
Babylonian and the Hebrew codes are the same.
A few salient points of likeness and unlikeness
in details will be given.

Slavery existed in both countries; but in the
Code of Hammurabi the term of servitude is
shorter, and if either of the parents is free the
children are free.

A son who strikes his father loses his hand in
the Babylonian law; he is put to death under
the Hebrew code.

Both codes exact the *lex talionis*—an eye for
an eye, a tooth for a tooth, etc.—but the Hammurabi code contains the unjust provision that

if a man strike a woman, and she dies, his own daughter shall be slain—a modified survival of the primitive conception that every member of a clan is responsible for the crime of one.

The Book of the Covenant contains the superstitious idea that a goring ox is accursed, and must be stoned to death.

Both codes direct that a thief caught in the act shall be slain; but the Hebrew law limits this penalty to robbery by night.

The Code of Hammurabi is superior to the Israelite legislation, in that it nowhere inculcates religious persecution.

Adultery and man-stealing in both codes are punished with death.

In both codes, if a man maim another accidentally, he shall pay for loss of time and the expenses of the doctor.

Both codes provide for equitable compensation when accidental injury has been inflicted upon the property of another.

False witness is vaguely condemned in the Hebrew legislation; but the Babylonian law inflicts severe penalties, amounting to death, if the suit be a capital one.

Authorities are not agreed on the originality of the Book of the Covenant. The resemblances to the Code of Hammurabi are very close ;[1] but they may conceivably have arisen from a likeness of conditions among peoples allied by

[1] See Chilperic Edwards, *The Hammurabi Code*, pp. 123-132.

blood and inheriting similar traditions. However, we have seen that the Hebrews borrowed many of their religious conceptions and observances from Babylonia, and this lends much probability to the opinion that their later ethics are not entirely independent of Babylonian influence. The morals of the age of David appear rather as a natural evolution. They bear the impress of crudity and barbarism. That they should be the result of many centuries of life in Babylonia and Egypt is inconceivable; but some elements of Babylonian culture may well have been derived from the Canaanites.

David behind the Ethics of the First Legislation.

It will not be needful to carry the development of Hebrew ethics beyond the age of the Book of the Covenant. How do the morals of David compare with the standard expressed or implied in this code? I think he has not advanced so far. He lived some two or three centuries before the completion of the Book of the Covenant, and, as I indicated in my introduction, we should expect him to represent a phase of morals intermediate between the morals of the nomadic Israelites and those of a settled and partially civilised community. A few instances will show that this expectation is verified.

In David's age the nomad's law of blood-revenge was still in force, as we have seen, though the incident of the woman of Tekoa (p. 39) shows us that it could be modified by the royal will. This concession was probably made because the deed was not premeditated. It was a manslaughter, not a murder. In the Book of the Covenant the old custom was further modified. If the homicide was not intentional, the slayer might find refuge at the altar (Exod. xxi. 13–14).

The laws of property were clearly in a very inchoate state in David's age. This is shown, for example, in the Nabal incident. David had been acting as protector to Nabal's sheep; but when he demands blackmail, and it is refused, he threatens to perpetrate wholesale massacre, and is only restrained by Abigail's intervention. Had the Book of the Covenant been in force, Nabal's sheep would have been guarded by the law: "If a man shall steal an ox or a sheep and kill it or sell it, he shall pay five oxen for an ox, and four sheep for a sheep" (Exod. xxii. 1). In the settled social conditions implied in this and similar laws David's career as an outlaw would have been scarcely possible. Furthermore, his intended revenge upon Nabal suggests an unorganized state of society far removed from the comparative civilisation of the First Legislation. Absalom's outrage upon Joab's barley is on the same plane of conduct as David's.

The peaceful reign of Solomon was the beginning of better things. Trade and commerce tended to restrain violence, to soften men's manners, and to create a sense of the rights of property. A new morality came into being, and found its expression in the utterances of Amos and his compeers.

Division II.—DAVID'S PLACE IN THE ETHICS OF CONTEMPORARY NATIONS.

The Assyrians and Babylonians.

Boscawen[1] points out the difference in the dominant national ideas of Assyria and Babylonia. Istar, who in Assyria is a goddess of war, "best represents the life of the Assyrian nation. War was the life of the nation, its sole means of existence." The cylinders of dates ranging between 1120 and 625 B.C. are "one unending chronicle of bloodshed." But in Babylonia the Semite "found the outlet of his energies in trade." Another civilising influence was the Sumerian literature, which stimulated the intellect of the Semitic invaders, so that as early as 2300 B.C., and especially during the reigns of Hammurabi and his successors, "Babylon became as great a home of letters......as Baghdad was under the Abbasides."

We learn then that, more than a thousand years before David, when the Hebrews, if they existed at all as a nation, were little more than savages, Babylon enjoyed a comparatively high civilisation. The Code of Hammurabi proves that its laws were at least as just and equitable as were the laws of the Israelites some fifteen centuries later. The Assyrian culture in David's age, on the other hand, displays striking analogies with that of the Hebrews. David represents, on a small scale, warrior-kings like

[1] The First of Empires, pp. 27, 28.

Tiglath-pileser I. (circa 1120 B.C.) and Asur-nasir-pal (884 B.C.). He spends his time in extending his dominions by war, and he ascribes his success to the help of the national deity, Yahweh. So, too, Tiglath-pileser[1] associates piety with bloodshed. In one of his inscriptions he sacrifices a large number of animals " to my Lord Assur," he prays that Anu and Vul may preserve him in power, " support the men of his government, bring rain, make him victorious." Asur-nasir-pal,[2] whose reign was marked by cruelties exceptional even in his age, is a pious " worshipper of Anu, exalter of Yav." He conquers, " by help of Assur and Yav," and his deeds are " in honour of Assur, the Sun-god, and Yav,[3] the gods in whom I trust." Tiglath-pileser was zealous in repairing the temples of the gods, and Asur-nasir-pal rebuilt the temple of Istar. David, with equal piety, brought up the ark to Jerusalem, and proposed the erection of a temple to Yahweh. The inscriptions of these Assyrian despots tell us also of internal improvements, of the introduction of foreign animals and plants, and the construction of canals. But the Bible records no beneficent domestic reform in the reign of David. He built himself a palace, singing men and singing women enlivened his repasts, and luxuries unknown to the pre-monarchic age ministered to

---

[1] *Records of the Past*, v. 21.   [2] *Ibid*, iii. 42, 46, 49.
[3] If, as I have already suggested, Yav is the same as Yahweh—both are war-gods—David becomes a fellow-worshipper with Asur-nasir-pal.

his desires.   We are told that he attended to the administration of justice; but this was a necessary duty of sovereignty, and implied no superior moral character.   In truth, we find in David the ordinary qualities of an Asiatic despot of his time — valour in battle, cruelty in victory, treachery in diplomacy, and little regard to the rights of his people.   His religious fervour rose to no higher pitch than the zeal of Asur-nasirpal, and it exerted as little effect upon his moral conduct.   It did nothing to make him merciful to his enemies, beneficent to his subjects, or just to woman.

The Egyptians.

The morals of the ancient Egyptians are clearly set forth in the Book of the Dead, which came into use after 2000 B.C.   They indicate a higher standard than existed in Israel in David's time.   The following are some of the confessions of sin supposed to be made by a righteous soul in the underworld after death.   Standing before Osiris the Judge, he declares : " I have not done privily evil against mankind.   I have not afflicted persons or men.   I have not told falsehood in the temple of Truth......I have not made the labouring man do more than his task daily...... I have not been idle......I have not calumniated the slave to his master......I have not made to weep.   I have not murdered......I have not done fraud to men......I have not committed adultery. ......I have not falsified measures......I have not cheated in the weight of the balance.   I have

not withheld milk from the mouths of sucklings. ......I have not stopped running water."

The advanced ethics of the Egyptians is further apparent in the position of woman, who was " on a perfect equality with man, and occupied a higher position than she did in any other country of the ancient world. For example, a married woman could hold property of her own, and might lend from it to her husband upon good security, such as his house."[1]

Justice, so conspicuous in the treatment of women, was placed by the ancient Egyptians "far above prudence, fortitude, and temperance." Truth stood on an equally high level, and, according to Wilkinson,[2] mercy, love, hope, and charity, with justice and truth, were so highly esteemed as to be deified. How small a place these virtues occupied in the moral code of David we have already seen. Yet, in traditions which still linger among us, the law under which David lived and reigned was perfect and divine; while the name of Egypt stands for darkness and sin.

The superior morals of the Egyptians, as of the Babylonians, were due to their more advanced civilisation. The cultivation of the arts of peace in a populous and prosperous community creates new duties, and gives rise to a powerful public opinion, which embodies itself in custom and law. Life acquires a higher value, property is more carefully protected, and the exigencies

[1] *Enc. Bib.*, col. 1223.   [2] *Ancient Egyptians*, ii. 173.

of trade and commerce enforce a high standard of honesty and justice, without which an industrial community could not hold together. The social forces that develop higher morals are far too powerful to be materially affected by the speculations of theologians or the ritual of Churches. Religions change and pass; but where there is civilisation there must be morality, otherwise the civilisation perishes, and the social structure falls to pieces.

The Greeks.

It is probable that the Homeric poems describe the state of Greek society, somewhat idealized, in the time of David. The best modern writers date them at about 850 B.C.; but whether they were composed by a poet named Homer, or were at that time current in the form of anonymous songs preserved in the memory of minstrels, is not certain. At all events, it would seem that they were for the first time written down and combined by Pisistratus, the tyrant of Athens, in the sixth century B.C. They must, therefore, refer to times preceding Pisistratus by several centuries, and may be dated a little later than David's reign.

In these poems we see a vivid picture of Greek manners and morals. Sometimes gods are described, and sometimes men; but in character there is little difference between the mortals and the immortals. The latter are more powerful; they can slay on a larger scale; they can vanish and reappear; and they are generally invulnerable; but essentially they are men and women, with human vices and human virtues, the former predominating.

According to Grote,[1] the chief moralising forces of Homeric society were (1) mutual devotion between kinsmen and companions in arms, (2) hospitality to strangers, and (3) protection to the suppliant. These were also the chief distinguishing virtues of the Hebrews of David's age. Loyalty to friends and kinsmen is one of the earliest moral qualities, for it is a vital necessity of tribal and family defence against external hostility. David was endowed with warm social affections, and the same feelings are attributed to Esau and Joseph. Hospitality to strangers is a common virtue among nomads, and it was apparently practised by the ancient Hebrews, such as Abraham (Gen. xviii.), Lot (Gen. xix. 1–3), Laban (Gen. xxix. 13 f.), Reuel (Exod. ii. 20), Manoah (Judges xiii. 15), and the old man in Gibeah (Judges xix. 17–21). Notable among these examples is the hospitable loyalty of Lot, who is willing to make great sacrifices in protecting his guests from ill-treatment. The base treachery of Jael to Sisera is an exception; but here the fervid patriotism of the writer of the poem apparently confuses his moral perceptions. We may fairly conclude that the virtues of the personages described by the Yahwist, which are in the main the virtues of David's age, did not

---

[1] *History of Greece*, vol. i.

materially differ from those of the Homeric Greeks.

Their vices also were similar. The ferocious homicides of the Hebrew king, his massacre of helpless populations, and his harsh treatment of prisoners, are scarcely worse than the practices of the Greeks. David's mutilation of his slain Philistine foes is approached, though scarcely paralleled, in barbarity by the Greek heroes, as, for example, by the mutilation of the dead bodies of Hector and Deiphobus. His untruthfulness is equalled, perhaps exceeded, among the ancient Greeks. Mahaffy describes[1] Greek society as "full of guile and falsehood." The current code recommended openly that men should fawn upon their enemy until they got him into their power, and then to wreak their vengeance. The Greek gods are equally devoid of truth. Athene loves Ulysses because he is so deceitful. The same goddess lures Hector to his doom by assuming the form of his friend Deiphobus. She also conspires with Zeus, her royal father, to prompt the breaking of treaties solemnly sworn to. Zeus sends a lying spirit to deceive Agamemnon, just as Yahweh did to entice Ahab to his death at Ramoth-gilead.

The Greek heroes, like David, were freebooters. Achilles and Ulysses pillaged forcibly or by fraud. The men of their age regarded piracy as an honourable occupation. Grote remarks[2] that

---

[1] *Social Life in Greece*, p. 20 *f*.
[2] *Hist. Gr.*, i. 480.

"the celebrity of Autolykus, maternal grandfather of Odysseus, in a career of wholesale robbery and perjury, and the wealth which it enabled him to acquire, are described (in Homer) with the same unaffected admiration as the wisdom of Nestor or the strength of Ajax."

The sexual morality of the Homeric Greeks stood at a higher level than that of the contemporary Israelites. Women held a more independent position, and polygamy appears not to have been practised. Yet concubinage was in vogue, at least among the chiefs, and female captives were treated with as little respect as among the Hebrews of 1000 B.C.

Comparing Homeric society as a whole with the Hebrews of the same epoch, the balance of morality seems to turn in favour of the Greeks. They were superior in the externals of civilised life and in intellectual culture, and they appear to have advanced further in ethical attainment.

The Romans.

The earliest civilisation of Rome was marked by higher morals than the age of David. The blood-feud was suppressed at an early period by the authority of the State.[1] "The false witness was hurled from the Tarpeian rock, the harvest-thief was hanged, the incendiary was burnt." But the plunder of foreigners even as late as 509 B.C. was not considered censurable—a provincial form of morals which David certainly had

---

[1] Mommsen, *History of Rome*, I., 165, 166.

not outgrown.   The status of woman in ancient
Rome differed little from that which obtained in
the early Hebrew monarchy.   She was not a
person, but a chattel.   The Roman acquired a
title to a woman, " as to other moveables, by
the use and possession of an entire year."[1]   So
in Israel " the woman is the property of her
parents, and later on of her husband."[2]   In the
tenth commandment,[3] where a list is given of
the things which we must not covet, the man's
house ranks before his wife.   In later Rome
woman acquired a position of " great personal
and proprietary independence,"[4] such as the
Jew, and even his spiritual successor, the Christian, have not yet conceded to her.

DIVISION III.—DAVID'S PLACE IN WORLD ETHICS

Human nature all the world over is so similar
that, if we reproduce the environment of a people,
we to a certain extent determine its morality.
But we must take, not the environment of the
moment, but of an age.   By a political catastrophe, such as a foreign conquest or an internal
revolution, or by the emigration of a people to
another country, the external conditions acting
upon character may be suddenly changed; but
it may take centuries to produce a material
ethical effect.   Take the case of the French

[1] Gibbon's *Decline and Fall*, V., 392.
[2] *Babel and Bible*, p. 202.   [3] Exod. xx. 17.
[4] Maine's *Ancient Law*, p. 156.

Revolution. By a change so sudden as to amount to a cataclysm the French people were delivered from a dead weight of tyranny, injustice, and superstition. Their elastic minds at once rebounded into exaggerated forms of thought and desire, and there followed many years of mental and social instability. The ingrained habits of centuries could not be materially changed in a generation. The people have since been oscillating between a boundless liberty and a mediæval subservience to military adventurers. In truth, they are not even yet adapted to the large freedom which the Revolution gave them. And this instability is moral loss. When the French mind has grown to the dimensions of its wider environment, greater stability will come, and more solid moral growth.

Or a changed environment may cause degeneracy. A long series of circumstances forced upon the Spanish people a despotic government and a bigoted Church. Freedom of thought was repressed and almost extinguished. Originality, invention, enterprise, gave place to inanition and intellectual paralysis. The moral fibre of the nation shrank into servility, and righteousness degenerated into mechanical obedience to priestly law. The greatness of a people was destroyed by a contraction of its environment.

In my introduction I called attention to the transitional political and social conditions of David's age, and pointed out that the changed conditions produced ethical transformation.

Had the change been from the agricultural to the nomadic stage, morals would have suffered degeneration; but as the environment into which the Hebrews had entered was wider and more complex, the process was reversed; the morals of the people underwent an evolution. The operation of this law may be more clearly set forth by describing a modern nation in which ethical evolution is proceeding on lines parallel with those of the ancient Hebrews. Such an example will be more effective than one derived from history, because the facts are more accurately ascertained, and the personages appear more real. For my purpose, Afghanistan is, I think, the nearest to ancient Hebrewdom.

(a) David and the Modern Afghan.

The physical environment of the Afghan is not unlike that of the ancient Hebrew. His country is rugged and mountainous, without navigable rivers. The high lands are suited for pasture, the valleys for agriculture. Some of the Afghan tribes are still in the nomadic phase; but the settled population, like the Israelites in Canaan, are agriculturalists and warriors. Mechanical industries are unimportant, the people being largely dependent upon higher civilisations for the products of skilled labour. The Israelites of the early monarchy were equally backward, for even the magnificent Solomon could not build a temple to his deity without the aid of his heathen neighbours. The Afghans are dwellers, some in tents and some in houses.

This was also true of the Hebrews in David's time. The king himself refers to his residence in a "house of cedar" as exceptional; while Yahweh, his deity, "walked in a tent and in a tabernacle" (2 Sam. vii. 6). We may, therefore, infer that some of the Israelites of that age were dwellers in tents, as, of course, they had been before the conquest of Canaan.

The state of society in both ancient Hebrewdom and modern Afghanistan is, therefore, transitional between the frankly barbarous and the incipiently civilised. The chief industry is agriculture; but the advanced guard of the population has progressed to the skilled trades, while a residuum lags behind as nomads. The ethics of the two peoples is equally transitional. A few details will make this clear.

We have seen that in David's age the custom of the blood-feud was decaying. The new monarchy, working for the maintenance of its own existence and authority, aimed at the establishment of royal law, and this introduced a great civilising force, for the worst form of government is an advance upon anarchy. In the epoch of the Judges "every man did that which was right in his own eyes." The turbulent tribes, warring fitfully with each other and with external foes, presented a picture of society strikingly similar to Afghanistan up to the eighteenth century, when something like a settled form of government was established. But even at the present time the royal power is weak, and hardly reaches the clans inhabiting the more

remote districts. Tradition and custom are still
dominant. Private revenge is forbidden by the
Government, and preached against by the mol-
lahs;[1] but ancient habit is too strong for both
authority and religion, and the wilder Afghans
deem blood-revenge both lawful and honourable.
So, too, David condemned Joab's vengeance
upon Abner; yet he was unable to punish the
offender. He was also compelled by the force of
custom to surrender the descendants of Saul to
the revenge of the Gibeonites. The subjects of
the Ameer and of King David thus present to us
similar phases of opinion on the customary law
of the blood-feud.

Among the Afghans marriage[2] has ceased to
be a mere matter of bargain and sale, but the
usual price must be paid. The ancient Hebrew
law appears to have been scarcely so advanced
as this. Marriage by purchase was in full force.
The father of the bride sold her for a sum of
money to the father or other relative of the
bridegroom, and the consent of neither of the
principals was necessary. "To espouse," in
Hebrew, simply meant "to pay the price."
Human feeling, in course of time, sometimes
modified ancient custom. Rebecca's consent was
asked (Gen. xxiv. 58), though it was not required
by law. Rachel and Leah complained that their
father had appropriated to himself their purchase-money, instead of conferring it, or a part

---

[1] Elphinstone's *Account of the Kingdom of Cabul*, p. 166.
[2] Wake's *Evolution of Morality*, i. 375.

of it, upon them as a marriage-portion for themselves and their children (Gen. xxxi. 14–16). The bargain might be made directly with the prospective husband, as Laban with Jacob (Gen. xxix. 18 *f.*) and Saul with David (1 Sam. xix. 25), and these cases also show us that the bride might be purchased by service, peaceful or military. The practice of David himself was in entire accordance with the customs of his age. He took wives and concubines at his pleasure. How atrociously his concubines were treated both by his son Absalom and by himself we have already seen. One of the more barbarous of Afghan chiefs would hardly behave so brutally.

David's ideas of the rights of property were those of the more savage Afghan tribes, who are professed thieves. They think it a "matter of course to rob a stranger,"[1] but not with violence, unless he resists. David, as we know (1 Sam. xxvii. 8–12), could add lying and murder to his plundering raids.

The article on the Afghans in the *Encyclopædia Britannica* describes them as turbulent and unsubmissive to discipline, frank and affable, especially when they have an object to gain, capable of gross brutality, perjured, treacherous, vain, and insatiable, passionate and vindictive, quarrelsome and intriguing. There is scarcely one of these qualities which does not receive illustration in the heroes of early Hebrew

---

[1] Wake (quoting Elphinstone), *ibid.*, I. 369.

history, many of them in the character of David himself.

The virtues of the Hebrew and the Afghan are also similar. The Afghan, like the Israelite, is faithful to friends, kind to dependents, hospitable, protecting a guest even at great sacrifices, brave, hardy, laborious, frugal, and prudent.

The moral qualities of both Afghan and Hebrew are those of people who are emerging from a nomadic life and settling down into an organized community. They find themselves in an increasingly complex social environment, to which they must adapt themselves. The process is slow and interrupted; but it is sure. The transition among the Israelites was going forward in David's age, and three centuries later the moral progress was embodied in the teaching of the early prophets, Amos, Hosea, and Isaiah. But this ethical stage lies beyond the scope of the present work. The age of David saw the beginning of the decay of the virtues and vices of tribal life. With Amos and his compeers dawned the era of the morals of civilisation.

(b) David and the Ethical Ideal.

Most of the great religions have promulgated the ethical law that we should do to others as we would they should do to us. But within what limits? The principle is recognised, in a rough way, by some of the most savage peoples—within the clan; by many semi-barbarous communities —within the tribe; by the early civilisations—

within the nation. Not even in theory has the world advanced further than this. Would the Russian or the German extend it to the Chinese? Or the Briton to the Caffre? Or the American to the Pawnee? And practice lags far behind even this theory. We have not yet learned to extend the principle to our next-door neighbour.

In its most elementary form morality hardly extends beyond the family, as among the Esquimaux. But it broadens with the growth of civilisation. Among many savages the clan is the unit. Within the clan men have duties to each other; outside, all are enemies, and no duties are owing to them. Murder, robbery, lying, have a meaning inside the clan; outside they have none. Mutual interest and sympathy bind together the individuals of the community, and give rise to its moral code. If clans coalesce into larger units, social differentiation sets in, new rights and duties are created, and thus the simple moral laws of the clan are gradually elaborated into the systematized ethics of the nation.

Israel entered Canaan as a congeries of clans. They were slowly consolidated into a loosely compacted nation. In David's time the clan system was decaying, and morality entered into a transition stage. *The real David marks this point in ethical development.* But his death did not end the evolution. David still remained the nation's ideal. As the people grew more moral, they went on moralising their ideal. What in each age they thought David to be, that was what

their own ideal had become. And so when the
ethical ideal embodied itself in Jesus of Nazareth,
the ideal David was not unworthy to be accepted
as his ancestor and forerunner.

My task is ended. I have endeavoured to give
a perfectly impartial account of the character of
David. I have extenuated nothing; but I have
set down naught in malice.

WATTS AND CO., PRINTERS, 17, JOHNSON'S COURT, FLEET STREET, LONDON.

CPSIA information can be obtained
at www.ICGtesting.com
Printed in the USA
LVHW08s2105280818
588394LV00011B/1113/P